MW01222149

STACEY'S CHOICE:
MARGARET LAURENCE'S *THE FIRE-DWELLERS*

Canadian Fiction Studies

Additional volumes are in preparation

Stacey's Choice:
MARGARET LAURENCE'S

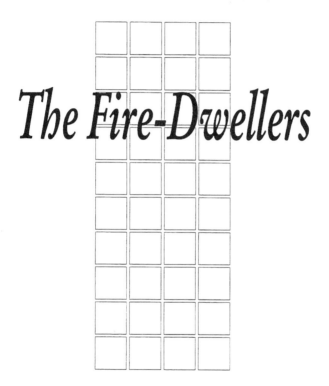

The Fire-Dwellers

Nora Stovel

ECW PRESS

CANADIAN CATALOGUING IN PUBLICATION DATA

Stovel, Nora Foster.
Stacey's choice : Margaret Laurence's The fire-dwellers

(Canadian fiction studies ; no. 24)
Includes bibliographic references.
Includes index.
ISBN 1–55022–127–2

1. Laurence, Margaret, 1926–1987. The fire-dwellers.
I. Title. II. Series.

PS8523.A8F537 1993   C813'.54   C91-095024-5
PR9199.3.L38F537 1993

This book has been published with the assistance of the
Ministry of Culture, Recreation and Tourism of the Province
of Ontario, through funds provided by the Ontario
Publishing Centre, and with the assistance of grants from
The Canada Council, the Ontario Arts Council, and the
Government of Canada through the Department of
Communications, and the Canadian Studies and Special Projects
Directorate of the Department of the Secretary of State of Canada.

The cover features a reproduction of the dust-wrapper from
the first edition of The Fire-Dwellers, courtesy of Thomas
Fisher Rare Book Library, University of Toronto.
Frontispiece photograph by Boult Photographics, Mississauga,
Ontario, reproduced courtesy of David Laurence.
Design and imaging by ECW Type & Art, Oakville, Ontario.
Printed and bound by Kromar Printing, Winnipeg, Manitoba.

Distributed by General Distribution Services,
30 Lesmill Road, Don Mills, Ontario M3B 2T6.

Published by ECW PRESS,
1980 Queen Street East,
Toronto, Ontario M4L 1J2.

Table of Contents

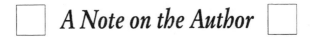

A Note on the Author

Nora Foster Stovel is Associate Professor of English at The University of Alberta, where she teaches modern British literature, as well as Canadian and contemporary women's fiction. She received the B.A., M.A., and Ph.D. from McGill, Cambridge, and Dalhousie Universities respectively, followed by Post-doctoral Fellowships at The University of Calgary. Nora Stovel has published numerous articles on modern British literature and contemporary Canadian and women's fiction in *Ariel*, *The D.H. Lawrence Review*, *English Literature in Transition*, *Essays on Canadian Writing*, *English Studies in Canada*, *The International Fiction Review*, and *Mosaic*, as well as in D.H. Lawrence, Margaret Drabble, and Margaret Laurence *Festschriften*. She has published *Margaret Drabble: Symbolic Moralist* (1989) and is currently working on *D.H. Lawrence: From Playwright to Novelist* and *Margaret Laurence, Diviner*. She has authored *Rachel's Children: Margaret Laurence's A Jest of God* for the Canadian Fiction Studies series and is composing *Wise Heart: A Biography of Margaret Laurence* for the Canadian Biography Series. Nora Stovel lives in Edmonton with her husband Bruce Stovel and their two children, Laura and Grant.

ABBREVIATIONS OF TITLES OF LAURENCE'S WORKS

BH	*A Bird in the House*
D	*The Diviners*
DCI	Donald Cameron Interview
DE	*Dance on the Earth*
FD	*The Fire-Dwellers*
"GG"	"Gadgetry or Growing: Form and Voice in the Novel"
GGI	Graeme Gibson Interview
HS	*Heart of a Stranger*
JG	*A Jest of God*
JQ	*Jason's Quest*
LDC	*Long Drums and Cannons*
SA	*The Stone Angel*
SJ	*This Side Jordan*
"TNV"	"Time and the Narrative Voice"
TT	*The Tomorrow-Tamer*
"TYS"	"Ten Years' Sentences"

Stacey's Choice:
Margaret Laurence's
The Fire-Dwellers

For my children, Laura and Grant

Chronology

1926   Jean Margaret Wemyss born July 18 in Neepawa, Manitoba, to Robert Wemyss and Verna Simpson Wemyss.

1930   Verna Simpson Wemyss dies. Sister Margaret Campbell Wemyss returns to Neepawa to care for niece Margaret.

1931   Margaret Campbell Simpson marries Robert Wemyss.

1933   Robert Morrison Wemyss born.

1935   Robert Wemyss dies.

1938   Margaret Simpson Wemyss moves with children Margaret and Robert to home of her father, John Simpson.

1939   Margaret Laurence's first story, "Pillars of the Nation," using name Manawaka, wins honourable mention in *Winnipeg Free Press Contest*.

1940–44   Attends Neepawa Collegiate, edits school newspaper, wins Governor General's Medal.

1944–47   Attends United College, Winnipeg. Publishes poetry and stories in college paper, *Vox*. Completes B.A. in Honours English.

1947–48   Works as a reporter on the *Winnipeg Citizen*.

1947   Marries Jack Laurence, war veteran and civil engineering student.

1949   Jack graduates from University of Manitoba. Laurences move to England.

1950   Laurences move to Somaliland, where Jack builds dams in the desert.

1952   Laurences move to Ghana. Daughter Jocelyn born.

1954   *A Tree for Poverty: Somali Poetry and Prose* published in Nairobi.

1955   Son David born.

1957	Ghana achieves independence. Laurences move to Vancouver. Laurence's stepmother, Margaret Simpson Wemyss, dies.
1960	*This Side Jordan* published.
1962	Margaret Laurence separates from Jack and moves to Hampstead, London with children.
1963	Margaret Laurence moves to Elm Cottage in Penn, Buckinghamshire, with children. *The Tomorrow-Tamer* and *The Prophet's Camel Bell* published.
1964	*The Stone Angel* published.
1966	*A Jest of God* published and awarded Governor General's Gold Medal.
1968	*Long Drums and Cannons: Nigerian Dramatists and Novelists 1952–1966* published.
1969	*The Fire-Dwellers* published. Laurences divorced. Writer-in-Residence at Massey College, University of Toronto. Purchases summer cottage on Otonabee River near Peterborough.
1970	*A Bird in the House* and *Jason's Quest* published.
1971	Companion of the Order of Canada.
1972	LL.D. awarded by Trent University and Dalhousie University and D. Litt. by University of Toronto.
1973	Writer-in-Residence at University of Western Ontario. Returns to Canada. Sells Elm Cottage and buys house in Lakefield, Ontario.
1974	*The Diviners* published and awarded Governor General's gold medal. Writer-in-Residence at Trent University.
1975	Receives Molson Award for *The Diviners* and awarded D. Litt. by the Universities of Brandon, Mount Allison, and Western Ontario.
1976	*Heart of a Stranger* published.
1979	*Six Darn Cows* and *The Olden Days Coat* published.
1980–83	Chancellor, Trent University.
1980	*The Christmas Birthday Story* published.
1987	Died January 5 in Lakefield, Ontario.
1989	*Dance on the Earth: A Memoir* published posthumously.

The Importance of the Work

Margaret Laurence is "Canada's most successful novelist," according to *The Oxford Companion to Canadian Literature*.[1] Laurence's greatest accomplishment is her famous Manawaka series set in the mythical town of Manawaka based on her own home town of Neepawa, Manitoba: *The Stone Angel* (1964), *A Jest of God* (1966), *The Fire-Dwellers* (1969), *A Bird in the House* (1970), and *The Diviners* (1974).

The Fire-Dwellers is an important novel for several reasons: first, as one of Laurence's Manawaka novels; second, as a germinal feminist work; third, as an accurate record of an historical era; and fourth, as a pioneering postmodern text.

FIRST LADIES OF MANAWAKA: THE FAMILY OF WOMAN

"Margaret Laurence, First Lady of Manawaka" is the title of a 1978 National Film Board documentary. There are Manawaka ladies in fiction as well as in fact, if we consider the heroines of Laurence's novels — Hagar Shipley, Rachel Cameron, Stacey Cameron Mac-Aindra, Vanessa MacLeod, and Morag Gunn. These Manawaka ladies are all related members of a fictional family: literally related in some cases, each heroine plays one of the various roles of woman in the family — as mother, daughter, wife or sister. They even play cameo roles in each other's features.

The first Manawaka lady is the redoubtable Hagar Shipley, the nonagenarian matriarch of *The Stone Angel* (1964). Laurence calls Stacey Cameron MacAindra, heroine of *The Fire-Dwellers*, "Hagar's spiritual grand-daughter" ("TYS" 22), suggesting a spiritual inheritance that is confirmed when Stacey prays, "Give me another forty years, Lord, and I may mutate into a matriarch" (281).

Stacey Cameron MacAindra is literally the sister of Rachel Cameron, heroine of *A Jest of God*. Laurence explains, "In *The Fire-Dwellers*, Stacey is Rachel's sister (don't ask me why; I don't know; she just is)" ("TYS" 21). Opposing personae of the author perhaps, the two sisters are opposite in personality — Stacey seeming the jovial extrovert and Rachel the neurotic introvert. Examples of "the road not taken,"[2] the sister novels may represent opposite choices for women, for the sisters have gone in different directions: Stacey has escaped the manacles of Manawaka to marry Mac MacAindra and live in Vancouver, while Rachel resides in Manawaka with their aging mother May over the Cameron Funeral Parlour. With classic sibling rivalry, each woman envies her sister, thinking the grass is greener on the other side of the Rockies. Laurence comments, "Each sister envied the other for what each imagined was an easier life than her own" (*DE* 176).

The sister novels are set in the same summer, as Stacey and Rachel both endure turning-points in their lives. Estranged for seven years, the sisters are *en route* to reunion. Writing the sister novels was an exercise in point of view for Laurence too, as each woman must learn to empathize with her sister and view her with charity. Laurence's emphasis, as always, is on the importance of love as compassion, as each of her solipsistic protagonists develops from claustrophobia to community. "Only connect"[3] is a tall order, but one that Laurence believes in.

The two sister novels are sibling texts in practical terms also: published consecutively in 1966 and 1969, the works were composed simultaneously, since Laurence interrupted Stacey's story to tell Rachel's tale and then returned to complete Stacey's narrative. Laurence explains, "Stacey had been in my mind for a long time — longer than Rachel, as a matter of fact" ("TYS" 22). Sister novels technically too, both works employ parallel epigraphs, opening nursery rhymes, and central patterns of imagery, as well as similarly schizoid narratives.[4]

Stacey Cameron MacAindra is also a schoolmate of Vanessa MacLeod, heroine of Laurence's short story collection *A Bird in the House* (1970). Vanessa mentions Stacey in her narrative, while Stacey mentions Vanessa in hers. Like Stacey Cameron and Margaret Laurence herself, Vanessa MacLeod grows up to leave Manawaka, although she carries it inside her skull for as long as she lives, just as Laurence did (*HS* 4). Ghosts from Manawaka haunt Stacey too, including the Tonnerre family, who reappear in *A Bird in the House* and later in *The Diviners* (1974).

Stacey Cameron MacAindra is also a schoolmate of Morag Gunn, heroine of *The Diviners*. Stacey plays a cameo role in Morag's narrative, and Morag's life develops many moral themes embedded in Stacey's story. A technical *tour de force*, *The Diviners* also employs many postmodern techniques of narrative and structure that Laurence develops in *The Fire-Dwellers*, for Stacey's memories become Morag's "MEMORYBANK MOVIES" and her fantasies become Morag's fictions.

FEMINIST FICTION: HOUSEWIFE AS HEROINE

Before this century, novels tended to end either with marriage or death. Traditional tragic novels ended in death, and comic novels concluded at the altar, with hero and heroine destined to live happily ever after. The curtain came down finally, not even hinting that there might be life after marriage. Death is indeed an end, but marriage is a beginning of a new communal life. Not until the sixties, with writers like Margaret Laurence, Margaret Drabble, and Doris Lessing, did novelists explore the realities of marriage and motherhood.

The Fire-Dwellers is an important early example of the new anti-heroine. Laurence says, "[Stacey's] not particularly valiant (maybe she's an anti-heroine), but she's got some guts and some humour" ("TYS" 22). An Everywoman, Stacey is the most ordinary of mortals, a middle-aged, middle-class housewife. No heroine in the usual sense, Stacey shows how truly heroic a person must be to survive in the modern world.

Laurence is an implicit feminist in all of her fictional writing, but in her nonfiction writing, most recently in her posthumously published memoirs, *Dance on the Earth* (1989), she declares herself explicitly a feminist (4), transforming the traditional terms into "herstory" and our "foremothers" (19).

Stacey is a prime candidate for the consciousness-raising of the seventies' women's liberation movement. Her husband Mac reveals sinister, perhaps sadistic, sexual tendencies: "That night in bed he makes hate with her, his hands clenched around her collarbones and on her throat until she is able to bring herself to speak the release. *It doesn't hurt. You can't hurt me"* (150). But it does. And he can. Stacey acknowledges the double standard: "He can and you can't" (22).

Stacey realizes that she is trapped in this marriage because of her economic dependence and her responsibility to her four children: "How could you walk out on him, Stacey, whatever he did or was like? You couldn't, sweetheart, and don't you forget it. You haven't got a nickel of your own. This is what they mean by emancipation. I'm lucky he's not more externally violent, that's all. I see it, God, but don't expect me to like it" (114). She thinks, "Wouldn't it be strange if I could ever stop thinking in terms of *them* and *me*?" (189). But can *they*?

Identity, particularly female identity, became a major theme for fiction in the sixties, especially in novels by women. Somebody's wife, somebody's mother, somebody's sister and somebody's daughter, Stacey wonders who the hell she is, to borrow her own idiom. Stacey's quest, like that of so many heroines of the period, is to salvage her self from beneath the layers of roles she is required by society to play — to resurrect the spirit from beneath the social construct.

Marriage involves motherhood, another new subject for the novel in the sixties. Mothers became scapegoats during that period, as the article Stacey encounters in a magazine suggests: "Mummy Is the Root of All Evil?" (277). The counterculture of the sixties created a generation gap that became a canyon. Stacey, a denizen of the beebop generation of boogie-woogie, is "a stranger in the now world" (274) of flower power and pot parties. This leads us to the third significance of *The Fire-Dwellers* — its vivid depiction of the cultural context.

CULTURAL CONTEXT: "DOOM EVERYWHERE"

The Fire-Dwellers is one of the most compelling chronicles of the sixties counterculture, one of the most fascinating eras in our recent history. Laurence captures the cultural context with vivid verisimilitude. She portrays the scene through the ever-open eyes of Stacey MacAindra, bemused and amazed by the world around her. Bombarded all day long by radio, television, and newspaper with news of fresh disaster, Stacey concludes, "*Doom everywhere* is the message I get" (58). Laurence explains, "[Stacey] is concerned with survival, like Hagar and like Rachel, but in her case it involves living in an external world which she perceives as increasingly violent and indeed lunatic, and trying simultaneously within herself to accept middle age with its tricky ramifications" ("TYS" 22).

In her memoirs, *Dance on the Earth*, and in essays collected in *Heart of a Stranger*, Laurence declares herself a pacifist and ecologist passionately opposed to war and nuclear arms and eloquently preaching peace, compassion and the salvation of our planet. *The Fire-Dwellers* is the first fictional work where Laurence confronts these contemporary problems explicitly.

PIONEERING POSTMODERNISM: "VOYAGE OF EXPLORATION"

The Fire-Dwellers is also a pioneering postmodern text, in which Laurence experiments with innovative techniques that prophesy her technical triumph in *The Diviners*. She shows how hard it is for the individual to salvage a unified sense of identity in the face of contemporary culture which fragments the self. Laurence develops innovative techniques for conveying the interaction between character and context. Her schizoid narrative method, counterpointing silent stream-of-consciousness monologue with spoken dialogue, portrays the personality trapped between the internal and external dimensions. The paradox of past and future is captured by her schematic use of memories and fantasies, triggered by the present. Techniques of the ever-open eye of television juxtaposing fictional violence with factual battles, radio broadcasts blaring death and destruction, and newspaper headlines screaming disaster conspire to create the contemporary context of the fire-dweller. Laurence's intertextual techniques, alluding to Greek and Christian mythologies, biblical and literary texts, extend her frame of reference from the contemporary to the archetypal. Just how far ahead of her time Laurence was in experimenting with such postmodern techniques will become apparent when we consider the critical reception of *The Fire-Dwellers*.

Laurence's artistry transcends technique, however, as the author strives to create "the kind of vehicle or vessel capable of risking that peculiar voyage of exploration which constitutes a novel" ("GG" 89). Through examining *The Fire-Dwellers*, we can discover how well Laurence has achieved her artistic ideal and how much she has contributed to the development of contemporary Canadian fiction.

Critical Reception

The Fire-Dwellers has not yet received either the critical attention it deserves or attention comparable to that paid to Laurence's other Manawaka works. Why has The Fire-Dwellers been so neglected by critics? Laurence was so far ahead of her time in both feminist content and postmodernist form that critics are just beginning to catch up. Only in the last decade has this novel begun to attract the critical attention it deserves. A review of its critical reception will tell us much about the novel *and* the development of Canadian criticism.

Reviews of The Fire-Dwellers can give us some clues. Laurence observed that "some of my work, particularly my novel, THE FIRE-DWELLERS, received some real put-downs from a number of male reviewers" (GGI 200). She reports, "Who on earth, I asked myself when I began writing this novel, is going to be interested in reading about a middle-aged housewife, mother of four? Then I thought, the hell with it — some of my best friends are middle-aged housewives; I'm one myself" ("TYS" 21–22). But many male reviewers appear enraged by the figure of the housewife as heroine.

Canadian male reviewers, including Frank W. Watt, in The Canadian Forum for July 1969, respect Laurence's reputation while disliking her recent production:

This book contains flaws enough to sink half a dozen books by lesser novelists. It survives because of the vitality of its central character, Stacey, the focal point of the action and the chief window of consciousness into the novel's world. This is a lot to entrust to a fictional character who is *merely* [my emphasis] a middle-class mother of four children, short, overweight, too broad-beamed to be fashionable, without intellectual, literary or artistic pretensions, and on the point of drowning in the familiar mess of mid-twentieth [sic] trivia. It has to be a tribute to Margaret Laurence's talent that we get caught up in Stacey's experience, find her needs and her weaknesses and her curiously innocent infidelities charming and troubling, and in the end learn to care about her and come to believe that what she thinks and feels and tries to do matters. (198)

Watt dislikes Stacey as "malicious and irresponsible," dismisses the subject-matter of midlife identity and marital crises as "the stale material of middle-aged marital tedium, loss of identity and motivation and sexual escapism," and concludes that "The ground occupied by *The Fire-Dwellers*, in both subject-matter and technique, is on the borderline between art and soap-opera. . . . The four walls of the room, or of the world have closed in too tightly. Margaret Laurence needs more breathing space than this for her genius to flourish" (198–99).

In "Face to Face," Margaret Atwood reports a conversation with Laurence:

Some male reviewers, [Laurence] feels, have given her books sexually biased reviews, and this was especially true of *The Fire-Dwellers*. "They found Stacey threatening. Hagar in *The Stone Angel* was an old woman, she was too far removed from them, and Rachel in *A Jest of God* was a spinster, you know, pathetic, they didn't have to worry about her. But Stacey was a wife and mother, and if their own wives and mothers had thoughts like hers they just didn't want to know about them." These reviewers didn't claim the book was a bad book: just one they didn't want to read. "You could sum up their attitude toward Stacey as, 'Why doesn't she pull herself together?' There was a lack of perception about the reasons that she couldn't." (37)

Canadian feminist reviewers, such as Phyllis Grosskurth and Diana Loercher, appear to appreciate *The Fire-Dwellers* more. Loercher applauds Laurence's depiction of the existential dilemma dramatized by a middle-aged, middle-class housewife:

The Housewife as Heroine, and not merely an adjunct to her Husband as Hero, appears to have been considered a subject of too paltry significance to warrant treatment beyond stories in ladies' magazines. . . . Miss Laurence evidently decided to risk the perils of inconsequentiality in deference to that neglected, unappreciated household drudge conventionally known as Mom, who might just have something to say after all, and more surprising still, might possess sufficient eloquence to express it. (203)

Appreciative of the feminist breakthrough demonstrated in the novel's subject-matter, however, Loercher fails to appreciate its pioneering postmodern form:

This novel is particularly impressive in its compassionate yet unsentimental depiction of human imperfection. Had Miss Laurence stopped there all would have been well, but she unfortunately fell prey to the infusion-of-meaning mania alluded to earlier. Instead of contenting herself with presenting a witty, perceptive, courageous, fallible housewife/mother/ woman coping with problems of truly awesome gravity in their own right, Miss Laurence seems to have feared that perhaps Stacey wasn't sensitive or worthy enough after all, so she interjected throughout the novel italicized recitatives about God, death, war, social injustice, etc., to up Stacey's awareness quotient. This pompous panorama is jarring enough when rendered in the form of newscasts, but coming from the mouth of Stacey it is ludicrous. For example, Stacey talks to God a great deal. This is a clever, credible device that is sometimes successful but more often painfully pretentious. Miss Laurence should nevertheless be commended for creating a character who is so alive that she defies betrayal by her creator. One feels that it is Stacey who is having the last, wry laugh on us all. (204)

Loercher's partisan view leads her, ironically, to be as condescending as Watt.

Phyllis Grosskurth, in a 1970 review entitled "Wise and Gentle" in *Canadian Literature*, comes the closest to appreciating Stacey's female identity crisis in trying to accommodate the contradictory constructions society imposes on woman:

The heart of Stacey's problem is that society forces so many roles upon her that she can find no clear line of continuity connecting one posture to another. By turns wife, mistress, mother, neighbour, all she knows is that she is expected to be beautiful, efficient, radiantly cheerful, and she is an abject failure in every department. (194)

While she sympathizes with Laurence's contemporary female protagonist, however, Grosskurth has definite reservations about the novel's artistic resolution: "The novel ends in unresolved compromise." She explains, "If this wider view seems somewhat arbitrarily imposed as an artistic solution it is because Stacey has so completely dominated our interest from beginning to end of this wise, gentle book" (195–96).

Few reviews predict the artistic and linguistic appeal that recent critics have found in Laurence's most experimental Manawaka novel. D.O. Spettigue both comprehends the universal appeal of Laurence's creation — "Stacey is not only every woman but Everyman coming to terms with his inadequacies and at the same time learning his strength" — and also anticipates recent critical appreciation of Laurence's examination of language: "A book also about language, then, exterior ones, social ones, the intimate language of the body and especially the forever unspoken agonized language of the solitary self that is every one of us" (723–24).

An anonymous reviewer for *Booklist* for June, 1969, echoes this perception: "Meshing an inner dialog and external conversations impressively, Laurence creates Stacey MacAindra, a middle-aged Everywoman with whom women readers can identify and whom men particularly sensitive to literary craft can appreciate as another worthwhile addition to Laurence's growing portrait gallery of women." Men (and women) sensitive to literary craft are beginning to make themselves heard.

Kent Thompson, in his 1969 review for *Fiddlehead*, perceives the paucity of critical equipment to deal adequately with Laurence's postmodern techniques: "The writing which has appeared in the last year is clearly very fine writing. But it is clear also that we lack the critical equipment to deal with it. We have learned to deal with literature in terms of ideas, or in terms of symbol, or plot, or dramatic conflict. And these terms are clearly inadequate to deal with the sophisticated craft of achieved art" (73). Thompson predicts the future.

Subsequent critics of *The Fire-Dwellers* develop critical equipment to deal with Laurence's "sophisticated craft of achieved art." Discussions of the novel take three forms: introductions to New Canadian Library editions by Allan Bevan and Sylvia Fraser, chapters on the novel in book-length studies of Laurence's fiction by Clara Thomas, Patricia Morley and Jon Kertzer, and articles by Miriam Packer, Sharon Nancekevill and Cristl Verduyn devoted to *The Fire-Dwellers*. Let us review these discussions over the last two decades.

Accounts of *The Fire-Dwellers* in the seventies are few: only Allan Bevan's 1973 Introduction to the NCL edition and Clara Thomas's chapter in *The Manawaka World of Margaret Laurence* (1976) focus on it. Both discussions demonstrate enhanced appreciation of Laurence's themes and techniques. Both emphasize the essential humanity, rather than the implicit feminism, of the heroine.

Bevan's brief introduction remains one of the very best discussions of *The Fire-Dwellers*. In a few short pages, he clarifies character, theme, narrative method, and symbolism succinctly. Bevan appreciates Stacey's female identity crisis: "*The Fire-Dwellers* is a searching novel about life in the mid-twentieth century as seen through the eyes of a middle-aged, middle-class, ordinary sort of a woman who needs to remind herself that she should have an identity of her own, other than that of wife and mother" (210). But he observes that Stacey's desperate dilemma is echoed by her husband's: "Only near the end of the novel does Stacey appear to become aware of the strong probability that Mac's inner world is as tormented as hers. . . . We know Stacey's struggle, but we only see Mac's from her limited perspective. We come to sympathize with her because we see her inner torments of isolation, whereas we can only guess at Mac's private world of memories, prayers, fears, and uncertainties" (207–08). Unlike male reviewers of the novel, Bevan sympathizes with Laurence's female protagonist, and, unlike female reviewers, he admires Laurence's artistic achievement.

Clara Thomas's 1972 essay on "The Novels of Margaret Laurence" in *Studies in the Novel* introduces views that she develops in her 1976 book, *The Manawaka World of Margaret Laurence*: "It is Margaret Laurence's triumph and honour that she chose this woman, a middle-class housewife, chose to engage our sympathies for her — and succeeded," for "Her creator has endowed her unmistakably with a mind that requires our respect, an imagination that demands our effort to follow, and a heart and a spirit that demand our humility" (60).

Thomas's chapter on *The Fire-Dwellers* in *The Manawaka World of Margaret Laurence* echoes this essay by appreciating Laurence's pioneering feminism in creating the housewife as heroine in the figure of Stacey Cameron MacAindra: "Stacey is the third of the 'ordinary' women whom Margaret Laurence has challenged us to recognize as individual and extraordinary — Hagar, old and ugly; Rachel, neurotic spinster, self-obsessed; now the anxious, donkey-on-a-treadmill stereotype, the housewife-and-mother of our time" (115). Thomas admires Laurence's contemporary creation: "[Stacey] is everyman and everywoman in North American urban society: the media *must* be her message because there is no escape from them" (115). Thomas also perceives Laurence's technical achievement: "*The Fire-Dwellers* is technically the most complex of the three novels — a fast-shuttering, multiscreen camera and soundtrack technique. Margaret Laurence has described her difficulties in 'orchestrating' the whirling, kaleidoscopic facets of Stacey's mind and imagination, never static but desperation-impelled with energy" (124).

Not until the eighties do we find essays devoted to *The Fire-Dwellers*, including articles by Miriam Packer, Sharon Nancekevill, and Christl Verduyn, as well as Sylvia Fraser's Afterword to the new 1988 NCL edition of the novel, and chapters on the novel in Patricia Morley's *Margaret Laurence* (Twayne, 1981) and Jon Kertzer's *Margaret Laurence* (ECW, 1988). These recent accounts begin to appreciate *The Fire-Dwellers* both as a feminist text and as a pioneering postmodern work. Let us begin by considering the discussions in books.

Morley appreciates Laurence's feminist subject: "*The Fire-Dwellers* presents an ordinary housewife with whom many women will identify," as "Much of the action takes place inside Stacey's head as she struggles with herself, her husband, their four children, and their society, to wring a modified victory from besetting difficulties" (99). Morley observes that "*The Fire-Dwellers* points implicitly to the force of social conditioning on women's consciousness" (106), but judges, ironically, that "Without the irony of the narrative voices and the honesty of vision this material would be melodrama. As it is, the novel's ending parodies a serialized soap opera. . ." (99). Morley applauds the parodic element: "Laurence's wit and love of language runs throughout her work, but *The Fire-Dwellers* is perhaps her funniest novel, albeit the humor is black" (106). But ultimately

Morley disapproves of Laurence's mimetic techniques, concluding that *"The Fire-Dwellers* is weakened by unnecessary repetition, boring exchanges, and occasionally blatant symbolism. It might profit by deletions" (108).

Jon Kertzer's discussion of *The Fire-Dwellers* in *Margaret Laurence* is both perceptive and articulate. He analyzes the dilemma of identity in terms of the social construct of woman, tracing Stacey's journey of self-discovery through her narrative. Laurence's heroines "seek to establish the patterns that give their lives meaning, and they seek to narrate them," for "The two tasks, understanding and narrating (or giving voice to), are really the same" (35). Kertzer says that Laurence's metaphor of "Mental baggage suggests that life is a journey through time, that we carry with us the past and its burden of guilt, that the mind is an untidy, overstuffed container. But it also suggests that Stacey is strong enough to carry her bags. Unpacking them means reviewing, analyzing, judging — in short, composing the narrative that forms this novel" (37).

Articles on *The Fire-Dwellers* throughout the eighties project a sense of discovery and celebration — discovery of Laurence's pioneering feminism and postmodernism *and* celebration of the vitality of her artistic achievement. Miriam Packer's 1980 essay on "The Dance of Life: *The Fire-Dwellers*" celebrates the dance of life that Laurence uses as her major metaphor in her posthumously published memoirs, *Dance on the Earth*. Packer posits that "Laurence's women are psychologically paralyzed until they release themselves from the prison of rigid control and surrender to the call of their own inner lives, to their fiery and repressed passionate selves" (124). Perceiving that "Form is intricately related to content in this novel" (126), Packer explores the fire symbols and dance metaphors, celebrating Stacey's vitality in dancing amid the flames.

In "*The Fire-Dwellers*: Circles of Fire" (1984), Sharon Nancekevill employs the model of the cosmogonic cycle of Joseph Campbell's *The Hero with a Thousand Faces* to explore the cyclical structure of Stacey's quest and Laurence's novel. She traces Stacey's progress through the three stages of this monomythic journey to self-knowledge: separation, initiation, and return. Nancekevill demonstrates how the circular nature of Stacey's journey is reflected in the circular structure of the novel, demonstrating that a graphic representation of Stacey's memories, fantasies, and dreams reveals the overall cyclic nature of *The Fire-Dwellers*. She concludes that "Ultimately the heroine's quest leads to rediscovery of her inherent strength and recognition of her ability to cope in a world on fire by placing both herself and that world in proper perspective" (170).

Recent articles are more explicitly feminist. Christl Verduyn's 1988 essay on "Language, Body and Identity in Margaret Laurence's *The Fire-Dwellers*" claims that *The Fire-Dwellers* reflects a number of the predominant themes which have emerged in contemporary feminist writing and criticism, especially the female experience of reality, which is dissected in three ways: "physically (through the body), psychically, and in terms of human identity" (128). She claims that "Close examination of Laurence's *The Fire-Dwellers*, for example, discloses a subtext wherein language is repeatedly shown to be an inadequate vehicle of expression for the protagonist Stacey Mac-Aindra" (128). Verduyn examines "the extent to which *The Fire-Dwellers* contains a subtext illustrating three themes which dominate contemporary feminist critical thinking: language, body and identity" (129). She shows how Stacey struggles with the inadequacies of language, of the social construction of the female body and of the centred sense of the self as subject, as she attempts to develop a sense of identity that will accommodate her perception of reality. She concludes, "Margaret Laurence's *The Fire-Dwellers* suggests that there is a conjunction of language and identity in woman's understanding and expression of self" and presents an "interrogation of language and its constructs of the female body and human identity" (138–39).

Sylvia Fraser's Afterword to the 1988 NCL edition of *The Fire-Dwellers* celebrates the novel primarily as a pioneering feminist text: "In the spring of 1969, when *The Fire-Dwellers* was first published, women were beginning to express their sense of generic, no-name frustration, but had not yet found a confident social voice, and the words 'women's liberation' were just moving into general circulation" (283–84). Bringing our discussion of the critical reception full circle, Fraser cites Barry Callaghan's review of *The Fire-Dwellers* in the *Toronto Telegram* on May 3, the very day of publication: "Callaghan dismissed MacAindra's aching loneliness as 'the bleating of a dumb, starved, and boring lady of neither the night nor the day but of limbo.' For Callaghan, Stacey MacAindra was that most tiresome of creatures, an unattractive female, 'frowsy and flat-chested . . . a loser' " (284). Fraser concludes, "twenty years after the novel's publication, it is Callaghan's kind of review that seems 'bleating,' antiquated and 'of limbo' while Laurence's portrait of Stacey MacAindra shines through as a compassionate depiction of a woman caught at a particular time of her life, in a particular time of the female collective life" (285).

Fraser appreciates Laurence's postmodern technique in *The Fire-Dwellers*:

> Perhaps more than any other of Laurence's novels, *The Fire-Dwellers* partakes of its time. Using sophisticated techniques which allowed her to pass easily from past to present, from reality to fantasy, from interior monologue to exterior observation, incorporating bits from television newscasts, clips from magazines and movies, Laurence recreated the kaleidoscopic sixties as experienced by Stacey MacAindra — a world of housewives and of breadwinners, of plastic kitchenware peddled as party-ware and vitamin pills as immortality, of governments threatened by the fires of nuclear holocaust and morals by the flames of illicit sex. (284–85)

Let us see how Laurence recreates that contemporary world in *The Fire-Dwellers*. In so doing, we will disprove the reviewers who failed to appreciate Laurence's presentation of the housewife as heroine and the critics who failed to appreciate Laurence's experimentation with innovative postmodern techniques to recreate the protagonist's fractured consciousness and the fragmented cultural context.

Reading of the Text

CONTEXT: "WORLD ON FIRE"

Laurence has a gift for creating a context for her characters, and time and place in *The Fire-Dwellers* are both portrayed with vivid verisimilitude.

PLACE SETTING: "JEWEL OF THE PACIFIC NORTHWEST"

The setting of *The Fire-Dwellers* is like a whirlpool, with ever-widening circles spiralling out from the centre. Laurence uses setting the way a director of photography uses a camera, panning out from an interior to a wider panorama, as we look through the ever-open eyes of the central character Stacey MacAindra to the world in which she lives. We first meet Stacey in her own room in her house on Bluejay Crescent, the domestic interior of the novel, as she prepares to face the world. Stacey identifies with "the big dark-green frame house with gabled roof and screened front porch" (16), which is aging comfortably, as she is: "Stacey is attached to it, partly because she fears new houses and partly because her own veins and skin cells seem connected with this one" (32).

Stacey loves "its high-gabled grey shingled roof, its evergreen-painted cedar-shake-covered walls and its only slightly sagging screened veranda" (32), complete with old hammock labelled "The Anachronism," because it is like a second skin for her, part of her identity. In this comfortable family home she lives in uneasy proximity with her growing children, who sequester themselves behind their locked doors, and her husband, who inches so far away from her in their double bed that she is afraid he may fall out onto the floor.

This house which Stacey loves and Mac loathes represents the conflict between them. "This fortress, which I'd like to believe strong" (18), becomes a prison for Stacey, as she realizes that "My boundaries are four walls" (69). Eventually she realizes, "I was wrong to think of the trap as the four walls. It's the world" (276).

Laurence contrasts the MacAindras' unpretentious home with other interiors, from Thor Thorlakson's antiseptic modern apartment, through Tess Fogler's kitschy decor, to Luke Venturi's chapel in the forest. The interiors are extroversions of their owners' personalities — or extensions of their phoney façades.

Thor Thorlakson's apartment echoes the sinister luxury of Nero's Rome:

On the floor, a black-and-white fur rug looks as though it had been made from the skins of stillborn monkeys, softly eerie. The coffee table top is grey-veined marble. Voluminous white drapes are like the heavy fine linens of ancient Rome. On the walls, two abstract paintings in selected shades of orange, black and white. On a sideboard, a sharply orange vessel like a misshapen triangle in thin glass. The place is both ascetic and voluptuous. (39)

Tess Fogler's house on Bluejay Crescent is an apt setting for the Polyglam party, because it is a parody of plastic pretentiousness. Tess's taste runs to kitsch, which Stacey burlesques when Tess offers to exhibit her latest purchase: "Ten cuckoo clocks, forty-seven TV tables with puce-and-orange ballerinas prinking on them, two hundred packets of bath salts done up to look like dinosaurs and labeled *Hers* and *His*, five thousand hankies embroidered with pink tuberous-rooted begonias, and a partridge in a plastic pear tree" (77).

Tess creates the symbol of Bluejay Crescent in a sign depicting "a bluejay perched on a crescent moon. *Get it, Stacey? Bluejay Crescent. Cute, eh?*" (33–34). Stacey imagines a revolution on Bluejay Crescent, bastion of the bourgeoisie: "an underground movement. The Bluejay Crescent Irregulars" (82–83).

Luke Venturi's A-frame is the home of the counterculture, an architectural representation of an alternative lifestyle that Stacey longs for as an escape from the bourgeois conventionality of Bluejay Crescent: "Unpainted, the timber a cool light brown, it juts up among the green-needled trees and the welter of bushes like a small strange cathedral" (174). The interior echoes this note:

The room is filled with assorted junk — coarse-webbed fishnets in grey piles on the floor, the big smoke-green thick glass bubbles used as weights on nets, suitcases imperfectly closed and half spilling their underwear and shirts ... books outspread or dog-eared on a low table made out of a polished pine slab glowing and golden but with roughly tacked-on uneven do-it-yourself wrought-iron legs, somebody having got sick of the job of an artisan. The half-finished greystone fireplace has no mantel and bears deep eyeless cement pits where future hand-selected stones will possibly one day go. Ten-foot-high unhemmed and floor-trailing curtains of moss-green sackcloth veil the huge front window. An open and beautifully illustrated child's ABC rests on a rumpled loose-weave green and grey wool rug, Arabic-patterned. (163)

Stacey's reaction to these signs of culture and unconventionality is typically bourgeois — disapproving, but admiring: "Heavens. A semiclassy pad. If people have to safety-pin up the hems of their curtains — well. Okay, so a bourgeois I may be, but that kind of a slob I'm not. Still, all the books. What right have I to say? The hell with that. They're trying to intimidate me with the superiority of unhemmed curtains" (163). These conflicting signals confuse Stacey.

Panning out beyond the boundaries of four walls, Stacey's ever-open eyes observe Vancouver, "jewel of the Pacific Northwest" (10), in its splendid setting of mountains and sea. Stacey fears this city where she still feels a stranger after almost twenty years. Although Stacey broke the manacles of Manawaka years ago, she is still a "Small-town girl" (12) at heart — like her creator, who called herself "a small-town prairie person" (HS 18). Manawaka haunts Stacey in the form of ghosts from the past called Valentine Tonnerre and Vernon Winkler. Laurence states that "[Stacey] is concerned with survival" ("TYS" 22), and she suspects her children need a survival course to stay afloat in the urban swim: "Maybe the best thing would be to bring them up in the very veins of the city, toss them into it like into a lake and say swim or else" (12).

Stacey is drawn in ever-widening circles away from the suburban security of Bluejay Crescent into the dangerous maze of dockyards in the raffish area down by the waterfront. Laurence's descriptive powers are paramount here: "In the lobby of the Princess Regal

Hotel, some yawning yellow-toothed fishwife, flesh-wife, sagging guttily in a print dress sad with poppies, is sweeping up last night — heel-squashed cigarette butts, Kleenex blown into or bawled into, and ashes" (10). Laurence's sketches of the denizens of the docks are also vivid: "Ancient mariners tottering around in search of lifeblood, a gallon of Calona Royal Red. Whores too old or sick-riddled to work any classier streets. Granite-eyed youngsters looking for a fix, trying to hold their desperation down" (11).

This urban jewel is set in a magnificent ring of mountains, demonstrating the juxtaposition of civilization and wilderness that distinguishes Vancouver. Laurence contrasts city and country or civilization and nature in a traditional moralized landscape that suggests innocence and experience or even good and evil. Through the windows of her house, Stacey can see the mountains standing like city walls: "In the distance, the mountains form the city's walls and boundaries, some of them snow mountains even now, as though this place belonged to two worlds, two simultaneous seasons" (69). Like Shangrila, the silent snow-capped mountains beckon Stacey's spirit to a place of peace, suggesting a "death wish" (14).

The surrounding sea also inspires Stacey's imaginings of primeval mud and prehistoric monsters. She "can smell the sea, salt warmth and decaying seaweed, like the presence of some rank stinking turbulent primeval creature which has not yet realized the fact of its own passing" (43). She views the seagulls as "prophets in bird form" (13) scavenging from the rusty old freighters floating in the harbour like "monolithic ghosts, clanking and groaning" (13).

Stacey is drawn hypnotically towards the waterfront, where the seashore forms the boundary between her real world and her dream world. Vivid as it is, the actual setting pales beside the imaginary one. Stacey, the original fire-dweller, views the neon flares of the city as the flames of hellfire, with its "rearing neons in lightning strokes of color, jagged scarlet, blue like the crested heart of a flame" (43). She longs for the cool, redemptive waters of the Cariboo, recalling childhood innocence at Diamond Lake or marital bliss at Timber Lake. Stacey lives in her fantasyland as truly as she lives on Bluejay Crescent, where nightmares of forest fires vie with dreams of distant lakes. She fantasizes about a suburb of the spirit: "*Out there in unknown houses are people who live without lies, and who touch each other. One day she will discover them, pierce through to them. Then everything will be all right, and she will live in the light of the morning*" (85). Stacey longs for another place and time.

TIME SETTING: "THE NOW WORLD"

Time setting is just as important as place in the world of the fire-dweller. Laurence has caught the flavour of the sixties, one of the most fascinating eras in recent history. She portrays it not from the point of view of a revolutionary radical, strung-out dropout, or counterculture character, but through the ever-open eyes of Stacey MacAindra, middle-aged housewife, amazed and bemused by the world around her.

Frightened but fascinated by the sixties counterculture, Stacey explores the raffish waterfront, where poets and prophets rub shoulders with derelict winos, desperate junkies, and poxy whores. She wonders who lives in the dockyard maze:

Sandaled artists courting immortality and trying to scrape by in this life? Extravagant-voiced poets preaching themselves? Semi-prophets with shoulder-length hair, baubled in strings of colored seeds or glass, pseudo gemmery, maybe not pseudo for their purposes? Languid long-legged girls who speak a new tongue and make love when they feel like it, with whoever, and no regrets or recriminations? (70)

Stacey is "living in an external world which she perceives as increasingly violent and indeed lunatic" ("TYS" 22), Laurence says. Laurence emphasizes "the sense of anguish and fear which Stacey feels in bringing up her kids in a world on fire" ("GG" 87). Stacey worries about raising children in a drug culture. Headlines like "Seventeen-Year-Old on Drug Charge" lead her to imagine "Kids gaming with LSD — *look at me, Polly, I'm Batman* — *zoom* from sixth floor window into the warm red embrace of a cement death.... Granite-eyed youngsters looking for a fix, trying to hold their desperation down" (11). Stacey fears the drug culture is invading her family when adolescent Katie wants to see an experimental film called *Psychedelic Sidewalk*, and announces a date with a boy whose father reported him to the police for attending a pot party (274).

Behind the contemporary radicalism is the revolutionary fervour inspired by American military involvement in Viet Nam, which is compared to Niall Cameron's World War I and Mac MacAindra's World War II. Every day, the "Ever-Open Eye" portrays gruesome scenes of violence, making the news more disturbing than any Western serial, because "This time the bodies that fall stay fallen" (57):

EVER-OPEN EYE BOUGAINVILLAEA BURGEONING, EDGING STREETS WHERE BEGGARS SQUAT IN DUST. MAN BURNING. HIS FACE CANNOT BE SEEN. HE LIES STILL, PERHAPS ALREADY DEAD. FLAMES LEAP AND QUIVER FROM HIS BLACKENED ROBE LIKE EXCITED CHILDREN OF HELL. VOICE: TODAY ANOTHER BUDDHIST MONK SET FIRE TO HIMSELF IN PROTEST AGAINST THE WAR IN (116)

Stacey fears that her sons will be "Conditioned into monsterdom" (117), like the Viet Nam veteran who almost Karate-chopped his little sister. She feels for one mother photographed trying to pluck the burning Napalm from her baby's face and another mother photographed with open soundless mouth mourning the dead infant cradled in her arms (253–54). Stacey fears the violence will spread to her world.

Fanning the flames of paranoia is fear of the big bang. Nuclear holocaust threatens, when "the world ends not with a whimper but a bang" (179), to echo T.S. Eliot's "Hollow Men." Luke's science fiction novel, *The Greyfolk* (183–84), about the colonization of America by Africans after the Cataclysm, reinforces Stacey's fears. Laurence, horrified by the American bombing of the Japanese cities of Hiroshima and Nagasaki during World War II in retaliation for the Japanese bombing of Pearl Harbour in 1941, was a passionate pacifist who opposed nuclear weapons. When Stacey looks at the city of Vancouver, she suddenly sees the buildings "charred, open to the impersonal winds, glass and steel broken like vulnerable live bones, shadows of people frog-splayed on the stone like in that other city" (14–15). She recalls a television interview with a woman whose husband constructed a bomb shelter in their basement, as many people did at that time (58). Watching the news from Viet Nam, Buckle Fennick opines, "They oughta drop an H-bomb on them bastards" (57). Every day, the television news records bombings:
"EVER-OPEN EYE A HILLSIDE AND SMALL TREES SEEN FROM HIGH AND FARAWAY. THE SMOKE RISING IN ROLLING CLOUDS. VOICE: ACCELERATED BOMBING IN THE AREA OF" (116).

But violence is closer to home, as Stacey recalls recent American riots:

There was this newspaper picture of this boy some city in the States kid about twelve Negro kid you know shot by accident it said by the police in a riot and he was just lying there not dead but lying with his arm cradled up in a dark pool his blood and his eyes were wide open and you wondered what he was seeing. His parents cared about him as much as I do about my kids, no doubt, and worried about what might happen to him, but that didn't stop it happening. (178)

In "Open Letter to the Mother of Joe Bass," Laurence addresses the mother of the boy, "A Negro twelve-year-old" shot in the neck by police "by accident" (*HS* 201). Newspaper headlines declare the message, *"Doom everywhere"* (58). Stacey wonders, "Is it like that? All I know is what I read in the papers. . . . 'Girl Kills Self, Lover.' 'Homeless Population Growing, Says Survey.' 'Car Smash Decapitates Indian Bride, Groom.' 'Man Sets Room Ablaze, Perishes.'" (11).

No wonder peace marches were one of the most popular recreations of the day. Several novels written about this period, including Alison Lurie's *The War Between the Tates* (1974), David Lodge's *Changing Places* (1974), and Laurence's *The Fire-Dwellers* (1969), climax with peace marches. Stacey's fellow-marchers hold placards reading "WE REMEMBER HIROSHIMA" and "STOP THE WAR IN" (250); they sing "We Shall Overcome" (251) and "Where Have All the Flowers Gone" (252). But Stacey's march is an anticlimax when she realizes that Katie, not she, should be the marcher.

No wonder Stacey concludes, *"Doom everywhere* is the message I get" (58). Stacey's is a world on fire, and only in the deep well of the spirit can she find the redemptive waters that will fortify her for living in the flames.

CHARACTERS: "METHOD WRITER"

Laurence describes herself as a "Method writer" because she *becomes* her characters. She believes in "knowing the characters so well that one can take on their past, their thoughts, their responses, can in effect for awhile *become* them. It has sometimes occurred to me that I must be a kind of Method writer, in the same way that some actors become the characters they play for the moments when they are portraying these characters" ("TNV" 157). Laurence notes, "Stacey had been in my mind for a number of years. I almost knew too much about her and her family" ("GG" 86). But she insists, "Stacey isn't in any sense myself or any other person except herself, but we know one another awfully well" ("TYS" 22).

Laurence also respects the independent individuality of her characters, however:

> The character is not a mask but an individual, separate from the writer. At the same time, the character is one of the writer's voices and selves, and fiction writers tend to have a mental trunk full of these — in writers, this quality is known as richness of imagination; in certain inmates of mental hospitals it has other names, the only significant difference being that writers are creating their private worlds with the ultimate hope of throwing open the doors to other humans. This means of writing fiction, oriented almost totally towards an individual character, is obviously not the only way, but it appears to be the only way I can write. ("TNV" 157)

Character is the most important element of fiction for Margaret Laurence. She maintains that her characters virtually take her by the throat and demand to have their stories told. Composing her novels seems almost like taking dictation. Facets of the author's personality perhaps, each protagonist is nevertheless fiercely individual. Laurence respects the autonomy of her heroines, and her sense of moral responsibility as an artist is to portray her characters truly. In her Foreword to *Heart of a Stranger*, she writes:

> [F]or a writer of fiction, part of the heart remains that of a stranger, for what we are trying to do is to understand those others who are our fictional characters, somehow to gain entrance to their minds and feelings, to respect them for themselves as human individuals, and to portray them as truly as we can. The whole process of fiction is a mysterious one, and a writer, however experienced, remains in some ways a perpetual

amateur, or perhaps a perpetual traveller, an explorer of those inner territories, those strange lands of the heart and spirit. (*HS* 11–12)

STACEY CAMERON MACAINDRA: "HAGAR'S SPIRITUAL GRAND-DAUGHTER"

In *The Fire-Dwellers*, Stacey MacAindra née Cameron is the central character, for Stacey is the original fire-dweller. She is that contemporary phenomenon, an anti-heroine. Laurence writes, "[Stacey's] not particularly valiant (maybe she's an anti-heroine), but she's got some guts and some humour. In various ways she's Hagar's spiritual grand-daughter" ("TYS" 22). So ordinary as to be archetypal, Stacey is that most commonplace of mortals, the housewife. Middle-aged and middle-class, Stacey represents Everywoman. Laurence admires Stacey's "basic toughness of character, her ability to laugh at herself, her strong survival instincts" ("GG" 88). She emphasizes that "[Stacey] is concerned with survival, like Hagar and like Rachel, but in her case it involves living in an external world which she perceives as increasingly violent and indeed lunatic" ("TYS" 22). In *The Fire-Dwellers*, Laurence will show just how heroic the ordinary person must be, if she is to survive in the contemporary world.

In emphasizing the importance of character, the term Laurence repeatedly employs is *dilemma*, "because this matter of dealing with individual dilemmas seems to be my fate in writing" ("GG" 89). The word applies perfectly to Stacey, who is balanced precariously on the horns of her (or every mother's) dilemma — namely whether to live for herself or deny herself and live for her family.

Laurence portrays "Stacey's dilemma" ("GG" 87) through a dynamic of division between internal and external dimensions. Stacey's story is schizoid, because Laurence creates a counterpoint of viewpoints, alternating first- and third-person narrative techniques, switching from inside Stacey's consciousness to outside. Stacey also contradicts each actual utterance with a tacit comment introduced by a subtle dash: "These lies will be the death of me" (34), she fears.

Stacey is a split personality: she exclaims, "Help, I'm schizophrenic" (106), because "What goes on inside isn't ever the same as what goes on outside" (34), and it is always a shock to be transported "Out of the inner and into the outer" (161). The fine line between the two worlds threatens to break down, as Stacey's self-control wears thin. She writes two letters home to her mother, the actual one and an imaginary one, as she wonders "what would happen if just for once I put down what was really happening?" (138).

Seen from outside, Stacey seems to have everything going for her. If not the answer to the all-American (or all-Canadian) dream, her life is certainly rich and full. She is married to a responsible man, salesman Clifford MacAindra; she has four healthy children, Katie fourteen, Ian and Duncan ten and seven, and Jen two; she has a comfortable home, a "big dark-green frame house with gabled roof and screened front porch" (16), in the suburbs of Vancouver; and she is blessed with robust health and a reasonably secure income. What more could she want? Her sister Rachel Cameron, protagonist of Laurence's sister novel, *A Jest of God*, envies Stacey her ideal life: "Everything is all right for her, easy and open. She doesn't appreciate what she's got. She doesn't even know she's got it. She thinks she's hard done by, for the work caused by four kids and a man who admits her existence. She doesn't have the faintest notion" (*JG* 99). That's how much Rachel knows. The grass is always greener on the other side of the Rockies.

Stacey is well aware of her blessings — most of the time: she thinks, with characteristic self-mockery, "count your blessings, kid. Go ahead and do that. *I Was Pollyanna's Mum.* A ray of sunshine" (222–23). She loves her husband and her children — also most of the time. When God asks at the Day of Judgment, "*Stacey MacAindra, what have you done with your life?*" she will answer, "*Well, let's see, Sir, I think I loved my kids*" (14). She likes her house on Bluejay Crescent, so much that she does not want to leave even when Mac gets a bigger and better job, "because her own veins and skin cells seem connected with this one" (32) — "This fortress, which I'd like to believe strong" (18).

But at other times, the four walls seem like a trap to Stacey, and she is desperate to escape. An escape artist, she broke the manacles of Manawaka when she was only eighteen, emerging from the mausoleum of the Cameron Funeral Home, shaking the dust of the prairies from her feet and high-tailing it to Vancouver. After twenty years in this "jewel of the Pacific Northwest" (10), however, she still feels like a "Small-town girl" (12). Like Laurence, who calls herself "a small-town prairie person" (*HS* 18), Stacey is still a prairie girl who is never comfortable in a city. Now that she has resided in the sophisticated metropolis for nearly twenty years, however, she is frantic to escape to a cool lake in the Cariboo, or a silent snow-capped mountain beyond the city. Critic Miriam Packer summarizes Stacey's dilemma succinctly: "Stacey wants out; Stacey wants in" (127).

The way it feels to be Stacey MacAindra is very different from the way it looks from outside, however. Laurence emphasizes the importance of perspective through her narrative method, which alternates between internal and external points of view. Laurence introduces this dual inner/outer perspective on the opening page of the novel, as Stacey observes herself in the mirror, comparing the objective reality reflected there with her subjective self-image.

Stacey is thirty-nine, poised on the precipice of middle age. Moreover, she is launching into a classic mid-life crisis that Laurence's novel will chronicle. Stacey must accept the inevitable process of aging — "the question of a middle-aged woman having to accept middle-age and learn how to cope with the essential fact of life, which is that the process of life is irreversible" ("GG" 87).

On the opening page of the novel, "Stacey sees mirrored her own self in the present flesh" (8), compared with the wedding photograph of "Stacey twenty-three, almost beautiful although not knowing it then" (8). The mirror reflects "a jumble of her clothes, carelessly shed stockings like round nylon puddles, roll-on girdle in the shape of a tire where she has rolled it off" (7) — Stacey's spare tire? But the creature that emerges from this cocoon of clothing is no butterfly. Time has grown a ring of flesh around her waist, like the thick bark on aging trees: "Not flesh. Fat. F.A.T" (21). Inside every stout matron may be a slender sylph trying to get out. Looking in the mirror, she recalls "Stacey, five foot three, breasts like apples as it says in the Song of Solomon" (11).

On Stacey's body are printed the lines of time in the form of stretch marks etched across her breasts and stomach, "like little silver worms in parallel processions across my belly and thighs" (21), suggesting decomposition and putrefaction, the everlasting worm. Recalling her sylphlike self, Stacey reflects, "Five minutes ago. *Is* time? How?" (15). Time has become her enemy.

Stacey conceals her sylphlike self-image under the uniform of the suburban matron, putting on the social construction with its costume: "Stacey, who is shorter than she would like to be, is wearing her pale-blue last year's spring coat and, because her dark unruly hair needs doing, a small white veil-enfolded straw hat which she dislikes" (9). This costume can form a convenient façade: "Stacey, neatly and matronly dressed, her gloves in hand, adjusts the despised veil on her white straw hat, pulling it down over her forehead and eyebrows as though she intends it to act as a disguise" (131–32). When she makes love with Luke, Stacey wishes for "a kaftan with a small zipper" (187) to camouflage her middle-age spread and maternal stretch marks. Later she recalls with chagrin, "Stacey lacking any merciful robe" (189).

Stacey wonders how she appears to others, as she views herself from outside:

> —— What's she seeing? Housewife, mother of four, this slightly too short and too amply rumped woman with coat of yesteryear, hemlines all the wrong length as Katie is always telling me, lipstick wrong color, and crowning comic touch, the hat. *Man, how antediluvian can you get?* Is that what she's thinking? I don't know. But I still have this sense of some monstrous injustice. I want to explain. *Under this chapeau lurks a mermaid, a whore, a tigress.* (15)

Stacey is delighted when a workman, seeing her in Buckle's truck, takes her to be a whore: "I can't say to him, *Listen bud I'm a respectable married woman named thus.* Because here I'm not. They don't know what I am. They only see a woman in slacks and sweater, in the cab of Buckle's truck. My, my. Doesn't that seem strange. Do I mind? Am I offended? Hell, no. I'm delighted" (143).

Always a strong swimmer, Stacey fears she is out of her element in the fire of the city. She imagines herself a mermaid, an underwater creature longing for her natural element. Sometimes she feels she is drowning in the confusion of contemporary culture and frenetic family life: she envisions "*herself held underwater by her hair, snared around auburn-rusted anchor chains*" (34).

This division between internal and external selves is underlined by Stacey's name. "Stacey" is an abbreviation of "Anastasia," the name of the legendary daughter of the last Czar Nicholas, reputed to have escaped the Communist massacre of the Russian royal family in 1917. Looking deep into her own eyes in the mirror after someone called

Stacey a funny name, the young girl imagined herself as "Anastasia, princess of all the Russias; Anastasia, queen of the Hebrides, soon to inherit the ancestral castle in the craggy isles" (90). But the name Stacey also suggests *stasis*, the Greek word for stability, the *status quo*, which must be preserved at all costs. Her name also underlines her role as matron: "Mrs. Clifford MacAindra" is a far cry from "Stacey Cameron." She thinks defiantly, "I'm Stacey Cameron and I still love to dance" (124).

Names underline the theme of identity. Somebody's wife, somebody's mother, somebody's daughter, Stacey wonders who in hell she is, to use her own idiom. Somehow, in sixteen years of marriage and motherhood, the true Stacey has been mislaid. Will the real Stacey please stand up? *The Fire-Dwellers* chronicles Stacey's identity crisis, and the aim of the novel will be to rescue the real woman from beneath the layers of years, to unearth the true self from within the social construct — "Lady Lazarus."⁵ Luke asks his merwoman, "Who held you down? Was it for too long?" (166). He urges Stacey to "Come out. From wherever you're hiding yourself. See — if I look very hard, I can just about make you out in there, but miniature, like looking through the wrong end of a telescope" (167).

Stacey looks confident to characters like Tess Fogler, but she suffers from an inferiority complex about being overweight and uneducated: "Everything would be all right if only I was better educated. . . . Or if I were beautiful" (8). She is so beset by guilt, that she even feels guilty about worrying! "*Mea culpa*" (106) is her motto, suggesting a sense of original sin. Stacey, the original sinner, imagines that any misfortunes must be God's punishment for her crimes. Magazine articles fuel her paranoia: "Nine Ways the Modern Mum May Be Ruining Her Daughter" (17), "Are You Castrating Your Son?" (18), "Are You Emasculating Your Husband?" (55), "Mummy Is the Root of All Evil?" (277).

Stacey tries to set a good example for her children, but fails miserably. "I never swear in front of my kids. This makes me feel I'm being a good example to them. Example of what? All the things I hate. Hate, but perpetuate" (9). Luke chides, "What are you trying to be? A good example?" (167).

The children are getting on her nerves more than ever: "I'm getting so I can't stand uproar any more. I never used to be this way. Now one of the kids shrieks and I pounce, snarling" (14). Distraught by witnessing a car accident, she overreacts to a squabble between her sons and hurls them both to the floor in an unforgivable outburst of violence (19). She fears that she is becoming a "monster" (20) — "Conditioned into monsterdom" (117) by contemporary culture. "Overcome with shame at my spiritual acidity" (50), Stacey thinks, "I'm getting worse. I used to be nicer. If I live to be ninety, I'll be positively venomous. My grandchildren will flee from me in terror" (77).

Stacey's operative word is "cope" — something that she finds it harder and harder to do. Her mantra is *Everything is all right*" (8). She thinks that if she says it often enough, she will make it come true. When she cannot cope, she relies increasingly on the "Ritualized props" (275) of addictive substances — alcohol and nicotine. Addicted to gin and tonic, "Mother's ruin" (96), she gulps her drink, as if "she had just stumbled in from the Sahara" (47). She keeps "a gargantuan gin and tonic" (84) in "the deep concealing blue bowl of the Mixmaster" (48) — for emergencies, but "every other minute is an emergency" (128). Stacey reflects, "If I spent my life pouring myself full of vitamins and tomato juice instead of gin, coffee and smoke, maybe I would be a better person. I would be slim, calm, good-tempered, efficient, sexy and wise" (45) — all the qualities she aspires to but fails to achieve. An incurable "Optimist" (30), however, Stacey still hopes *Everything's all right*" (280).

Alcohol is responsible for the crisis when she burns her hand on the stove: "Two red crescent lines have appeared on the skin of her left palm" — "My brand of stigmata. My western brand. The Double Crescent" (130) — branding her like Christ. In her paranoia, she imagines that she has stigmata on her palms — the marks of the nails from the crucifixion: "I find I got stigmata on both palms and I gotta wear gloves everywhere I go" (101). Maybe that is why Stacey wears gloves and a hat and veil when she goes out — "Crucified Woman" (*DE* 15).

Eventually, Stacey becomes so desperate to escape from her dilemma that she contemplates suicide — the great escape. Ultimately, however, she learns to accept herself as she is, hips and all. Acknowledging, "The truth is that I haven't been Stacey Cameron for one hell of a long time now. Although in some ways I'll always be her, because that's how I started out" (276), she can accept her adult family responsibilities. She acknowledges that "in some ways

I'm mean as all getout. I'm going to quit worrying about it. I used to think there would be a blinding flash of light some day, and then I would be wise and calm and would know how to cope with everything and my kids would rise up and call me blessed. Now I see that whatever I'm like, I'm pretty well stuck with it for life. Hell of a revelation that turned out to be" (272). She can even accept middle age: on the eve of her fortieth birthday, the one she anticipated on the opening page of the novel, she falls asleep, praying, "Give me another forty years, Lord, and I may mutate into a matriarch" (281) — Hagar's spiritual grand-daughter indeed!

THE MACAINDRA FAMILY

Clifford MacAindra: "Agamemnon King of Men"

Clifford MacAindra, Stacey's husband, known as Mac, is introduced to us in the opening scene of the novel in the wedding photograph of Stacey with "Mac twenty-seven, hopeful confident lean, Agamemnon king of men or the equivalent, at least to her" (8). When he enters the scene in the flesh at age forty-three, Stacey does not think that he has changed much in sixteen years: "He is still as lean as ever, and although his auburn hair has darkened, he has lost none of it. He is still handsome to her. The main change is in the webbed lines around his eyes and on his forehead" (25). The equivalent of Stacey's stretch marks, Time's autograph, Mac's furrowed forehead inspires Stacey with guilt: she feels that she has laid a sword over his neck in the form of four children to support.

But everything goes way back, as Stacey (and the reader) learns. Son of a United Church minister, Matthew MacAindra, the only person on earth who calls him Clifford, Mac always felt the weight of responsibility for setting a good example. He has always felt guilty for not sharing his father's faith. A childhood anecdote that Mac shares with Stacey gives her (and us) some insight into his invisible burdens. Mac recounts an incident when he got mad and shoved his fist through the kitchen window. His father was furious, but didn't strap him. Instead, he *"Made me pray with him, for self-control"* (121), Mac recalls.

Stacey wonders, "What really happened? How was it for him?" She imagines:

39

Matthew, towering like Moses, bearing in his eyes the letter of the Law. Kneel down, Clifford, kneel down right here in the study with me, and we will both pray. Mac, longing for any whip rather than this one, knowing this occasion would never arise again, must not, looking at his father's clamped-shut eyes, listening to the flat voice calling upon the lord of all the galaxies to bear witness to a fragmented square of a brittle substance called glass by some of the users of it who lived on a small planet and who must learn not to break, not by not wanting to, but by some other reinforced and steel means. (121–22)

No wonder Mac has been conditioned to be the strong silent type, sporting the stiff upper lip of his generation of Canadian males. Mac carries more hidden baggage than Stacey can possibly imagine. But she begins to realize: "Maybe I do begin to see. If he doesn't deal with everything alone, no help, then he thinks he's a total washout. Thanks, Matthew — you passed that one on all right, but at least you had your Heavenly Father to strengthen your right arm or resolve, to put the steel reinforcing in your spine. Mac's got only himself. And if he doesn't speak of it to some extent, one of these days he'll crack up" (234).

Mac feels guilty for disappointing Matthew by not finishing university and entering a profession. Instead, he married and worked as a travelling salesman to support Stacey and their growing family. First he sold encyclopedias door-to-door, until one day he quit his job after refusing to sell *Once-Over World* to an "old retired logger, who wanted to see the picture of Piccadilly, London, where he'd once gone on leave in 1917 from the trenches" (24). Then he sold "essences" for Drabble's, perfumes and flavours with saccharine names like "Angel-Breath Mouth Freshener" and "Honey Blossom Garbage Tin Spray" (23) — a demeaning job.

Soon after the novel opens, however, Mac lands a new job with Richalife, selling placebos to chronic neurotics who hope that popping a pill will renew their psyches and physiques. Mac pretends to be thrilled, although secretly he thinks "it's a load of crap" (234). A sign of its unsuitability is Mac's new brush cut. Mac can't understand why his boss, Thor Thorlakson, needles him, although Stacey discovers that Mac has been *"scared by a strawman"* (245) from Manawaka. Later, Thor is transferred to the head office in Montreal, and

Mac is offered the position of regional manager (262). So everything ends happily ever after.

All the characters in *The Fire-Dwellers* are presented as couples in conflict, true to the dynamic of the novel. Stacey and Mac, the central couple, set the example. Married for sixteen years, their relationship has deteriorated drastically. Things are a far cry from Stacey's memory of their idyllic honeymoon at Timber lake when she said to Mac, "I like everything about you," and he replied, *"That's good, honey. I like everything about you, too"* (176).

Laurence portrays "the frustration of Stacey in trying to communicate with Mac" ("GG" 87), for all communication systems have now broken down. Stacey begs, "Oh Mac. Talk. Please" (26). She thinks, "Mac — let me explain. Let me tell you how it's been with me. Can't we ever say anything to one another to make up for the lies, the trivialities, the tiredness. . ." (25). All their conversations are like Theatre of the Absurd dialogues expressing lack of communication.

Mac has "started to go underground, living in his own caves" (24). Escaping the flames of family life, Mac becomes a cave-dweller, closeting himself in his study "amid his business files and racing car magazines and *Playboy*" (60). "He finds his exit where I can't follow and don't understand" (30); Stacey reflects, "whatever the game happens to be, it's a form of solitaire for Mac" (44). The couple's communication gap is sexual as well as verbal: "in bed he makes hate with her, his hands clenched around her collarbones and on her throat until she is able to bring herself to speak the release. *It doesn't hurt"* (150).

Parenting provides a major source of the couple's conflict. Afraid that some "unnatural flowering" (28) will turn his son into a "pansy" (29), Mac does "his sergeant-major act, the toughening process" (28). He chastizes Duncan for crying over an injury, and blames Stacey for babying him when he has nightmares. He shouts, "Ruin them, for all I care" (198), making her feel like a "Kid-ruiner" (29). The present contrasts with Stacey's memory of Mac visiting her in the hospital after Jen's birth, bringing her two dozen yellow chrysanthemums and saying, *"You did well"* (25). Mac redeems himself in Stacey's eyes when he cradles the almost-drowned Duncan to his breast and gives Ian three priceless words of praise, "You did fine" (269) — like Mr Ramsay in Virginia Woolf's novel *To the Lighthouse*.

Stacey finally appreciates Mac's idiom of silence, the stiff-upper-lip code of communication: "That's the most Mac will ever be able to say" (269). Stacey reflects, "The silences aren't all bad. How do I know how many times Mac has protected me by not saying?" (264). Finally, she even sees through Mac's façade: "Mac has to pretend he's absolutely strong, and now I see he doesn't believe a word of it and never has" (260). Laurence notes Stacey's "ultimate realization of [Mac's] bravery and his terrible hangups in having to deal with his problems totally alone" ("GG" 87). Stacey concludes, "Yet he's a whole lot stronger than he thinks he is. Maybe they all are. Maybe even Duncan is. Maybe even I am" (260).

Matthew MacAindra: "Moses, Bearing in His Eyes the Letter of the Law"

Matthew MacAindra, Mac's father, a retired United Church minister named for the Apostle, is a patriarchal figure, *"towering like Moses, bearing in his eyes the letter of the Law"* (121). "Upright to the point of unbearability" (47), Matthew is actually more vulnerable than he appears on the surface. Gradually, his true self is revealed, as the layers of his façade are stripped away.

"Matthew, always so neat and so proud" (256), is fastidious as ever, but has taken to carrying a black silver-topped cane (151), emblem of his fragility. A widower for eighteen years, Matthew is alone in the world, with Mac's family his only link, since his married daughter lives half a continent away. As a retired clergyman, he feels useless, although the new minister is "painstakingly cordial" (64).

Stacey knows she should invite Matthew to live with them, but the way he dogs her footsteps in a "gauche ballet" drives her into a "teeth-grinding fury" (254), nearly spurring her to "speak the unspeakable" (272). She reflects, "I know we ought to have him here. Don't tell me, God. I know. But when I think of it, I think — *mental hospital, here I come*. Following me around from room to room, desperate to make talking sounds, someone else who'd have to be told everything is all right" (65–66). Stacey's dilemma is driving her to drink.

Matthew irritates Mac and the kids as well as Stacey. He fusses at the kids and nags at Mac about not finishing university and not attending church (66). "Matthew's Sabbath quiz" (67), a Sunday school catechism that causes the kids to cringe, is one of the novel's running gags, as each Sunday more of them desert Sunday school to participate in Mac's Sunday car-washing ritual.

Matthew, who represents religion, makes everyone feel guilty — Mac because he cannot share his father's faith (258) and Stacey because she cannot see the world as Matthew does — "God's in his heaven all's right with the world" (63). Her guilt flares when Duncan draws spaceships rather than the Stations of the Cross on his Sunday School picture of Saint Francis (68). But Matthew inspires Stacey to sing a hymn and to shed her first tears, when he repeats the Psalm, "*Save me, Oh God, for the waters are come in unto my soul*" (152).

Matthew is not as infallible as he seems, however. His vulnerability is revealed dramatically when he falls down the stairs one Sunday, forcing him to "accept the unacceptable" (255) and confess that he has glaucoma. Confessing his physical weakness leads him to acknowledge spiritual weakness as well.

Matthew confesses to Stacey religious doubts that he has never acknowledged before: "Stacey, I always wanted to talk about it to someone, but I couldn't. I wish now that I had talked of it. Not to Mac, but perhaps to my wife" (257–88). He feels guilty for his doubts and for demanding that Mac have the faith he lacked: "But with Mac I failed. Perhaps there is something contagious about doubt. He must have known all along about that essential flaw in me" (257).

This new insight into "Matthew's despair" (257) prompts Stacey to call him "Dad" — the name reserved for her own long-dead father, Niall Cameron. Matthew's fall, sign of his fallibility, finally prompts her to invite him into her home: "Listen, Dad. You can't live there any more. Not now. Not with this. You'll live here. With us." She thinks, "Oh Christ, will I ever regret it. . . . It'll be pure bloody murder." Realizing she will have to escort him upstairs to the bathroom, she reflects, "If you think it'll be awful for you, doll, how do you think he'll feel about it? Matthew, who doesn't even like to admit he has any natural functions. Matthew, always so neat and so proud" (256).

The MacAindra Children: "Flame-haired Young Foxes"

Stacey and Mac have four children — Katie fourteen, Ian and Duncan ten and seven, and Jen two. All the children sport the same family emblem, the MacAindra red hair in shades of auburn — colour-coded

43

for life. Just as all of Laurence's protagonists represent facets of their creator's character, so the MacAindra children represent aspects of their parents' personalities: Katie demonstrates parallels with Stacey and Ian with Mac. The children both parallel the conflict between the parents and inspire it, as Stacey and Mac have opposite philosophies of child-rearing, Mac being the disciplinary and Stacey the permissive parent.

Katie MacAindra: "Fire Green As Grass"[6]

Katie is a younger version of Stacey, reminding her middle-aging mother of her own youthful, slender self, and making her feel like a frump in comparison: "Katie, baby, how can you be so gorgeous? I love you for it, but it makes me feel about a thousand" (67). Katie is symbolized by green, the colour of new growth: "She is wearing a dress the startling color of unripe apples, and her long straight auburn hair looks as though she has ironed it, which she has. No lipstick, but green eye make-up" (16).

Mother and daughter are like a before-and-after advertisement: Katie is a bud on the brink of blossoming into womanhood, while Stacey is poised on the verge of middle age. The before-and-after contrast is highlighted when Stacey dances secretly in an attempt to recapture her long-lost youthful self and then glimpses Katie dancing alone: "Katie is dancing. In a green dress Katie MacAindra simple and intricate as grass is dancing by herself. . . . Her bones and flesh are thin, plain-moving, unfrenetic, knowing their idiom" (127). Stacey reflects, "You won't be dancing alone for long, Katie. It's all going for you. I'm glad. Don't you think I'm glad? Don't you think I know how beautiful you are? Oh Katie love. I'm glad. I swear it. Strike me dead, God, if I don't mean it" (127).

Mother and daughter conflict, as the adolescent Katie attempts to establish her independence. When Stacey forbids Katie to see an A (for Adult) experimental film called *Psychedelic Sidewalk*, Katie accuses her of being "unreasonable, inconsistent and immoral" (46). Stacey can hardly miss the parallels with her own adolescent rebellion and begins to see the mother-daughter conflict from her own mother's point of view for the first time in her life. She can understand Katie's viewpoint too, although Katie cannot yet understand hers. The parallels appear ironic when Stacey returns from a tryst with her lover: Katie confronts her in stern judgment, warning, "Just don't ever bawl me out again, eh?" (168).

Names are significant in the novel. A sign of Katie's growing estrangement from Stacey is the fact that she has taken to calling her "Mother." As Katie matures, however, her sympathy develops. Their shared concern for Jen's trauma with Tess prompts a reunion: "Stacey recognizes all at once the way in which she and Katie have been talking. *We.* They have never before encountered one another as persons. At the same time, Katie has been unwittingly calling her *Mum* instead of *Mother*" (192). Katie reveals deep faith in her mother's capability: she says, "you would've known what to say. You always do. I never do." Stacey reciprocates by replying, "I don't always, either. Sometimes I think I hardly ever do" (192).

Ian and Duncan MacAindra: Cain and Abel

Ian and Duncan take after their father and mother respectively, echoing their parents' conflicts. Ian is a replica of Mac: at ten years of age he has inherited his father's stiff upper lip, whereas the seven-year-old Duncan is more open and expressive, like his mother, and will talk to her. Stacey watches them walking to school: "Ian walks ahead, as usual, slim and wiry, tall for ten, impatient, moving with a quick grace, perfectly in command of his muscles. Duncan rarely hurries, and is largely unaware of other people. Yet he will tell Stacey what he is thinking, sometimes. Ian guards himself at every turn" (17–18).

When Duncan has a nightmare or cuts his hand, he cries for his mother, whereas Ian, when upset, holds himself inclenched, his face white with fury. "Ian does not cry. His pride sometimes permits him stomach cramps, but never tears" (19). Mac commends Ian's rigid self-control and criticizes Stacey for indulging Duncan, fearing that her babying will result in his "unnatural flowering" (28) into a "pansy" (29). "Real men don't cry" is Mac's motto.

Ian and Duncan are opposites, Duncan a dreamer, Ian a man of action. The artifacts they produce express their natures. Stacey finds in the garage loft, where Ian likes to hide out and write (as Laurence did herself as a child), an old scribbler titled "Captain Ian MacAindra His Direy of How We Beat Enimy" (20). Duncan "draws pictures of the shark-shaped rocket which will one day take him to Mars or

Saturn, and of the scarlet forests he will walk there, under the glare of innumerable purple suns. He puts them away, and sometimes digs one out and looks at it with amusement as the product of an earlier self. But he never destroys them" (19). Stacey discovers Duncan in the basement twirling the dials on the washing machine, pretending it is a spaceship. Ian, in contrast, builds a model car with old boards and wheels and then destroys it in a fit of temper.

Like all brothers, including Cain and Abel in the Bible, Duncan and Ian fight like cats and dogs, reminiscent of the sibling rivalry between the Cameron sisters, Rachel and Stacey. Their animosity flares when Duncan unintentionally botches Ian's bug. "The fury rises until at last Stacey is unable to bear their battle and their noise. Cain and his brother must have started their hatred like this" (19). To her horror, Stacey involuntarily flings both boys to the floor. Ian loses control for once and hurls his bug down the basement stairs, declaring, "The hell with it then! I don't give a damn!" (19) — recalling the way Mac as a boy drove his fist in a fury of frustration through the kitchen window (121).

Ian does cry once, though. Duncan tells Stacey that Ian bawled after he chased a ball onto the street right in front of a car, recalling the death of his friend Peter Challoner, who was killed by a car at the opening of the novel. Realizing that Ian, unlike most children, knows that he's going to die, Stacey rushes to comfort him, but Ian cries, "*Can't you just leave me alone?*" (198), hurting her with his cruel echo of his father's very words. Stacey's attempt to protect Ian's privacy impels Mac to declare, "Ruin them, for all I care" (198).

Like all the other pairs of characters who conflict in the novel, however, Stacey and Ian are eventually reconciled, as are Ian and Duncan. Ian signals his forgiveness for Stacey's earlier unwarranted violence: after she comforts Duncan "trapped in his nightmare" (28) — which she feels sure was brought on by her outburst — Ian reaches out his hand to her in an uncharacteristic gesture (29). When Ian complains of a stomach pain as Stacey is desperate to leave home for a tryst with her lover Luke, Stacey reassures him and leaves (204). Returning home late, plagued by guilt from her ladybird conscience, she is greeted by Mac's words, "Stacey, he's dead." Stacey collapses, "speaking the one mourning word. Ian Ian Ian . . . ." When Mac reassures her, "Stacey — it's not Ian. . . . It's Buckle" (211), Stacey realizes how much she loves her elder son.

When Duncan, Stacey's favourite, almost drowns, it is Ian's presence of mind that fetches the lifeguard who saves Duncan's life by giving him mouth-to-mouth resuscitation, thus cementing a lifelong bond between the brothers.

Jennifer Rachel MacAindra: "The World's One and Only Nontalking Opera Star"

Jennifer Rachel, named Rachel for Stacey's sister, but called Jen, is the youngest child, Stacey's "flower." Appropriately, Mac brought Stacey flowers, two dozen yellow chrysanthemums, when she was born (25). But Jen is responsible for Stacey's trap, since she must stay home to tend Jen — flower power. Occasionally Tess Fogler, Stacey's next-door neighbour, baby-sits for Jen. An extroversion of Stacey's own vulnerability, for children are hostages to fortune, Jen suffers a trauma when Tess forces her to watch one goldfish kill and eat another (191).

The problem is that, at two years old, Jen still does not talk, but merely babbles in "garbled gargling" (273), symbolizing the communication breakdown in the MacAindra family. The novel opens as Stacey recalls the *"Ladybird, ladybird / Fly away home"* nursery rhyme she recited to Jen in an effort to teach her "a few human words" (7). Tess remarks, "My, she's determined not to communicate, isn't she?" (9). Jen does warble melodies, making her "the World's One and Only Nontalking Opera Star" (69). The eventual breakthrough in family communications is celebrated when Jen turns to her mother near the end of the novel and asks casually, "Want tea, Mum?" Rejoicing, Stacey thinks, "it's like brass bands and banners to me," and says, "Flower, you're a genius," but worries, "Ye gods. What if she never learns to say anything else?" (273).

THE CAMERON FAMILY: MANAWAKA GHOSTS

Niall Cameron: Manawaka Mortician

Niall Cameron, Stacey's dead father, was the town undertaker in Manawaka, proprietor of Cameron's Funeral Parlour, where Stacey lived with her family above the mortuary. But Niall was an alcoholic as well as a mortician, "capable only of dressing the dead in between bouts with his own special embalming fluid" (11). Stacey's main legacy from her father is the addiction to alcohol: when she returns to Manawaka for her father's funeral, she selects his flask from the Great War as a memento, reflecting, "Okay, Dad. Here's looking at you. You couldn't cope, either" (157). Niall Cameron was a veteran of World War I, but he refused to talk about it, merely drowning his memories in spirits (10). Stacey's two mementos from her father are both souvenirs of the war: a flask and a revolver — firewater and firearms, appropriate for a fire-dweller.

Following the funeral, Stacey penetrates the mortuary for the first time, observing "bottles once booze mixed with the jars and potions of a profession old as the pharaohs" (215), and drinks a libation to his spirit in a mickey of rye. Later she realizes that it is not the dead who deserve to be mourned, but the living dead — people like the zombie Niall Cameron, who die spiritually long before they die physically. Nevertheless, Stacey cannot call Mac's father "Dad," because that title is still sacrosanct to Niall Cameron (65). When she eventually does call Matthew MacAindra "Dad" (256), it signifies that she has finally laid to rest the restless ghost of her father, just as she has ultimately rejected death by drowning his revolver in Timber Lake.

May Cameron: Whining Widow

Stacey's widowed mother May is still alive, living in Manawaka over the funeral parlour with her single daughter Rachel. But she too is a ghost haunting Stacey with her whining voice and conventional platitudes, such as, *"It's not how you look, it's what you are that counts"* (21). When Stacey looks in the mirror, she can still hear the "soft persistent mew from upstairs, the voice that never tired of saying how others ought to be and never were," repeating, *"vanity isn't becoming"* (21), as she regarded Stacey "more in sorrow than anger" (46), like the ghost of Hamlet's father. Although Stacey has escaped her mother's manacles, she has internalized her attitudes as her conscience or superego.

Stacey's long-distance relationship with her mother is marked by letters — the one she writes, telling decorous hypocrisies, and one she considers writing, telling the truth. At the end of the novel, Stacey receives a letter from Rachel announcing that she is moving to the coast with their mother. Stacey jokes to Mac, "Maybe my mother will strike up a rewarding relationship with your dad." Absorbing her initial shock, Stacey acknowledges, "Well, it'll mean a lot to her to see the kids. I can't begrudge her. She's had her troubles. As I know now" (277). As a mother herself, Stacey can now see things from her mother's point of view.

Rachel Cameron: "Sisters Under the Skin"[7]

Stacey's sister Rachel has taken the other road from Stacey, returning home from university in Winnipeg on the death of her father to look after her ailing mother, who "plays guilt like a violin" (Atwood 214). Fourteen years later, she is still teaching school in Manawaka and living with her mother over the family funeral parlour. Stacey thinks, "Good-bye to Stacey's sister, always so clever. (When I think you're still there, I can't bear it)" (12). Neither can Rachel. She tells her own story in Laurence's preceding novel, *A Jest of God* (1966), which bears such interesting parallels with its sister novel, *The Fire-Dwellers*.

Although Rachel and Stacey have not seen each other for seven years at the outset of each novel, by the end of each narrative they are en route to reunion, since Rachel has finally broken out of her chrysalis and taken wing for the coast. Sisters under the skin, they may finally be able to forgive each other for living.

FRIENDS AND NEIGHBOURS: MIRROR IMAGES

Just as Laurence's heroines reflect aspects of their creator's character, so the minor characters reflect facets of the protagonist's personality. Stacey (from the Latin word *stasis* meaning stability, as in *status quo*) is the hub around which all the other characters turn, from her family to her friends. Like Stacey, all the characters wear a façade of confidence but prove very vulnerable under their veneer. All the minor characters are wounded because they have lost their families, and they all gravitate to the MacAindra family for stability.

49

Buckle Fennick: Kamikaze Trucker

Buckle Fennick is Mac's wartime buddy from World War II. Twenty years later he is still hanging around, dropping in at dinner time. Buckle has the swarthy ethnic good looks of most male sex objects in Laurence's Manawaka novels, including Nick Kazlik in *A Jest of God* and Jules Tonnerre in *The Diviners*: "he is stocky with muscular hair-flecked arms. He has a face like an Iroquois, angular, and faintly slanted dark eyes. His hair is night-black and straight" (48).

Buckle is the stereotypical macho man: "Buckle can swagger while standing still. He wears a sleazily shiny sports shirt, cerise and silver, and jeans" (48) — skin-tight and bulging at the crotch. His outfit matches his job: "Buckle is a trucker. He drives a diesel dinosaur, a steel monster, innumerable great tires, heavy as a mountain, roaringly full of crazy power. Buckle loves it. It is his portable fortress, his movable furnace. It is his lover and himself all in one" (50). Buckle drives his truck up the Cariboo and Alaska Highways through the "wheeling metallic ballet" (213) like a "Bat outa hell" (218).

Buckle is like a mediaeval knight riding his noble steed out to tilt with dragons — except the monsters he fights are those of his own subconscious. He plays chicken with other drivers, confident that "Nothing can happen to me while my luck's in" (51). He is "super-stitious as a caveman," although his "shrines are invisible" (52). His favourite game of Russian roulette on wheels may express a suicidal impulse. Eventually he gets his death wish.

Playing the hard-hat stereotype to the hilt, Buckle makes his idiom fit his macho image, borrowing his lines from "Old B-grade movies": invited to dinner, he replies coyly, "Twist my arm," and offered a drink, he responds daintily, "Don't mind if I do" (49). Uncle Buckle calls Jen "the champion pisser of the neighborhood" (50), and his solution to the war in Viet Nam is to "drop an H-bomb on them bastards" (57). Retelling the tale of how he missed one trucker by "a cunt-span" (143), he threatens to make another driver strum his *"motherfuckin' harp"* (51). But Buckle's bark is worse than his bite, as Stacey learns.

Stacey is ambivalent about Buckle: she thinks, "I detest him," but she also thinks, "he's sexy" (48). Rivals for Mac's affections, they are conscious of "the many unspoken small malices between us in our years of competition for Mac" (48). But Stacey is "overcome with shame at my spiritual acidity" (50) when she mocks Buckle. Surprised by sympathy, she realizes how vulnerable he is (59).

Stacey is right, for there is another, more vulnerable, side to Buckle, revealed by his full Christian name, Arbuckle, which he loathes and which only his mother uses — a sign of his concealed Achilles heel. His mother herself is one of his vulnerable points, as Stacey learns when she accompanies Buckle home to his apartment over Honest Ernie's in Grenoble Street near the dockyard, where "Stacey's eye camera" (145) records "The undersea giant woman" (147):

> The woman is gigantic, outspread like rising dough gone amok, swelling and undulating over the stiff upholstery of the chair, gaping body covered with tiny-flower-printed dress huge and shroud-shaped, vastly numerous chins trembling eel-like separate but involved, eyes closed, and at the end of the Kodiak arms, contrasting hands neatly made, fine-fingered, encrusted with silver-and-gold-coloured rings which might almost have been costly, from the way the hands flairfully wear them. (145)

Blinded by acid thrown in her face by another whore, Mrs. Fennick sits all day pouring port out of a teapot into a pink-pearl opalescent glass mug (145).

Like most of the minor characters in the novel, Buckle has lost his family. His wife, Julie Kazlik (sister of Nick Kazlik, Rachel's lover in *A Jest of God*) of Manawaka, introduced Stacey to Buckle's war buddy Mac (53). Then Julie left Buckle, taking their two-year-old son with her. Stacey will soon find out why.

Buckle invites Stacey to ride in his truck one day and then asks her home. Desperate for love and deprived of sex, Stacey is "Almost Ready for an Affair" (49) and fantasizes about sex with Buckle (141). But Buckle reveals an unexpected kink: an onanist, he prefers masturbation, with a woman as "witness to the agony of his pleasure" (147). Hurt by Mac's apparent admiration for Thor, Buckle has devised the ideal revenge, "a two-edged sword" (148): he tells Mac that Stacey went to bed with him, a fabrication which might almost be true, but which Stacey can never disprove. Later, Stacey surmises to Mac, "I don't guess he was all that interested in women, Mac. That was why Julie left him. He liked it with himself but with somebody looking on." She suggests, "Maybe he wanted you" (219).

Buckle plays chicken once too often and gets his death wish in a head-on collision with another diesel. Stacey accompanies Mac on his midnight visit to the mortuary — "chapel of the violent dead holding its eternal hours, crash and stab not knowing nine to five" (214) — to identify the broken body of *"Buckle Fennick, prince of the highway, superstitious as a caveman, Buckle who could swagger standing still, now lying stilled once and for all"* (217). Buckle's death proves a turning-point in Mac and Stacey's marriage. Unmanned not so much by Buckle's death as by the fact that he still named Mac as his next of kin on his identification, even after their recent quarrel over Stacey, Mac weeps for the first time, speaks at last, and admits his need for Stacey, holding her tightly, "blind to Bluejay Crescent, holding her not for her need now but for his own" (213).

Mac tells Stacey a wartime tale that gives her the key to unlock Mac's bond to Buckle. After the war in Italy, Buckle drove recklessly across a mined bridge that exploded. Mac saved Buckle's life, but realized that "I hadn't done him any favor" (219). Perceiving why "you had to take him on for life," Stacey absolves Mac of responsibility for the life and death of Buckle Fennick by assuring him, "You're not God. You couldn't save him" (219).[8] Surprised by sympathy for Buckle, Stacey weeps in a belated "requiem for a truck driver" (239).

Thor Thorlakson: "God of Thunder"

Thor Thorlakson is Mac's new boss, the district manager for Richalife, a program peddling pills as redemption:

> *Richalife — Not Just Vitamins — A New Concept — A New Way of Life.* With testimonials. *Both Spirit and Flesh Altered. Richness Is a Quality of Living.* Singing ads on local stations, blond angelic trilling. Rallies. Gimmicks falling like the golden shower of stars from fireworks. (34–35)

The Richalife program proclaims itself as the new religion, aping Christian ritual and Greco-Roman decor. Its confessional quizzes probe the personality's anxieties and deficiencies, goals and guilt (60–61). And its rallies read like religious rituals, with pseudo-hymns sung by choirs of angelic blonds:

The plastic lady's product, Polyglam Superware, a transparent alias for Tupperware, consists of "plastic vessels gleaming softly, pearl-pink, mauve, green like the pale underthighs of a mermaid, blue as pastel as angel veins" (80). These plastic wares are purveyed at parties in private homes, where the Plastic Lady plays word games, "the nicest fun thing ever" (80), with the name of her product, *Polyglam Superware*, shares recipes for "Tropical Paradise," a *"tummy treat"* for "toddlers and teens" (81), and dances in stiletto heels with "lake-water blue" plastic dishpans for waves (82) — a synthetic Botticelli Venus.

Valentine Tonnerre: Manawaka Ghost

Manawaka catches up with Stacey in the form of Valentine Tonnerre, a ghost from the past — almost literally, since she confesses that she is about to go on a long trip — "the last one" (242). Valentine materializes out of thin air: "Stacey hears, strangely, her name being spoken by a woman's voice, a voice raucous as the gulls' " (239). But the apparition looks real:

> Coming towards her is a woman whose black hair has been upfrizzed until it resembles the nest of some large wild bird. Her dark eyes and her features are prairie Indian but not entirely. Her skin, or what can be seen of it under the thick crust of make-up, is a pale brown. Her mouth has been lipsticked into a wide bizarre cupid's bow. (239)

Like all the characters in the novel, Valentine is an "expert at conceal-ment" (241), her facial makeup forming a literal façade, a false happy mouth painted over her real sad one, like a comic mask superimposed on a tragic one. Named Valentine, a man's name, because she was born on February 14, she does deserve a cupid's bow for a mouth, but hers is twisted askew with wry irony.

Valentine is a scion of the Manawaka Tonnerre family which plays a central part in *The Diviners*. A Métis family, their name means thunder. And indeed Valentine does debunk Thor Thorlakson, the phoney god of thunder (243–44). Valentine recalls the death of Piquette and her children when the Tonnerre family shack caught fire. Stacey makes the connection with her own recurring nightmare:

"Piquette and her kids, and the snow and fire. Ian and Duncan in a burning house" (241). Later, Stacey thinks: "Even her presence is a reproach to me, for all I've got now and have been given and still manage to bitch on and on about it. And a reproach for the sins of my fathers, maybe. The debts are inherited and how could the damage ever be undone or forgiven?" (241).

Luke Venturi: Counterculture Catalyst

The catalytic character in most Manawaka novels is a man from a different ethnic background with whom the heroine has an affair which provides her with a sentimental education. The catalytic character in *The Fire-Dwellers* is Luke Venturi, a young man who materializes beside Stacey at the seashore at midnight. In the depths of her despair, upset by Mac's suspicion that she has gone to bed with Buckle, Stacey runs away from home and heads, as always when in need of spiritual sustenance, straight for the sea. Luke fears she intends to drown herself, and he does save her from going under spiritually, if not physically.

Luke belongs to a different cultural background in more ways than one. An Italian dressed in an Indian sweater with Haida totems of eagle wings and bear masks, he is also a counterculture type, with uncombed too-long hair and an incipient beard, dressed in paint-splashed cords and off-white sweater, who has the gift of "looking at things from some very different point of view" (164).

When Stacey demands to know what he does for a living, Luke explains that he works on boats when he needs money or cooks in a logging camp. When he can, he writes — "Science fiction. SF. Not space opera with sex. Allegory, more, and all happening on this planet" (166) — paralleling Stacey's own SF fantasies and Laurence's own allegories. Luke's novel about *The Greyfolk*, which "Takes place some thousand or so years hence, when this continent is all desert and the few remaining people are governed by African administrators who followed the First Expedition which was sent from Africa centuries after the Cataclysm here, when the radiation danger had finally disappeared, to see if there were any survivors" (183–84), is particularly pertinent to Laurence's socio-political satire.

Luke's Christian name, recalling the Apostle, suggests his redemptive role. A sometime fisherman, like his biblical namesake, he is also a fisher of souls. What he offers Stacey is sympathy and salvation. He hears her confession (165) and offers her the wine of communion (183) — playing the priestly role of Murray Lees with Hagar, the father confessor figure in *The Stone Angel*. Stacey confesses her science fiction fantasies and her suicidal impulses, her family frustrations and guilt feelings. She even confides to him about her father's revolver and her final drowning it in Timber Lake. Once she has told Luke, she is able to tell Mac. Luke teaches Stacey to speak and to love, even herself, giving her "the gift of tongues" (*JG* 26). She finds herself addressing him in her mind and echoing his idiom, "Hey, how about that?" (195). After she learns to love with Luke, she can truly make love with Mac for the first time in the novel.

Luke's setting is appropriate for his spiritual function, for he lives in a timber A-frame that penetrates the forest "like a small strange cathedral" (174). The child's ABC lying open on the Arabic-patterned rug, like a Bible in this chapel in the woods, completes Stacey's spiritual education. Filled with fishnets and moss-green sackcloth curtains, the A-frame resembles a grotto or lagoon where Stacey experiences the spiritual sea change she has envisioned. Appropriately, Luke calls Stacey "merwoman" (166), recalling her own self-image of a mermaid (15). Preparing to return to the chapel in the woods, Stacey dons a dress painted in blues and greens, "like seawater and fir trees" (174).

Luke's surname, Venturi, suggests adventure, and his travels to unknown territories up north are exciting to Stacey. Like Othello with Desdemona, Luke tells Stacey terrifying tales of travel and adventure. He has visited farflung Indian settlements with "the totems of the dead" (208) reflected in his Indian sweater with its Haida motifs of "outspread eagle wings and bear masks" (162).

Luke offers to fulfil Stacey's escape fantasy by inviting her to share that adventure, to accompany him up north to Kitwanga, where the ferry over the wild Skeena River is driven by an old man resembling "Charon" (208), the legendary figure who ferried dead souls across the River Styx to the underworld in ancient Greek religion. Stacey is tempted by the vision which reflects her death fantasy: *The totem poles are high, thin, beaked, bleached in the sun, carvings of monsters that never were, in that far dusty land of wild grasses, where the rivers speed and thunder while the ancient-eyed boatman waits* (222). Faced with a choice, Stacey decides, "I can't leave. . . . I have to go home" (209), prompting Luke to repeat the Ladybird nursery rhyme for the second, and pivotal, occasion.

Luke is like "the shadow prince" in *A Jest of God* (19), offering, if not "tea and sympathy," then "coffee and sex" (206). Every housewife's fantasy figure, he listens and loves, with no strings attached, assuring Stacey that "You're not alone" (165), that real mothers do cry, that everything really is all right. Like all fantasies, of course, he's "not *that* real" (165), as Stacey realizes when she learns that she is literally old enough to be his mother. Fortified by fantasy come to life, Stacey can go home again to cope with her realities, for Laurence believes that "You have to go home again" (*The Diviners* 324).

Delores Appleton: "Girl from a Medieval Tomb Carving"

After Stacey confesses her sexual encounter with Buckle Fennick, Mac admits that he has had a brief love affair with Delores Appleton. One of Thor's golden girls, Delores dresses like a vestal virgin or Delphic oracle in white toga-like tunic with Greek key design. Looking like "a girl from a medieval tomb carving" (136), Delores (meaning "sorrowful" in Latin) is one of the walking wounded. Her address at the Richalife rally is really a confession of pathetic dependency. When Mac admits that "she really needs to be cared about by some guy over a long time," Stacey thinks, "Like I have been, by you, come hell or high water" (220–21).

MINOR COUPLES: MIRROR IMAGES

The other minor couples in the novel, the Foglers and the Garveys, are like mirror images of the major couple, Stacey and Mac. Tess and Jake Fogler reflect the central relationship in a sinister manner.

Tess Fogler: Perfectly Packaged

Tess, the neighbour who babysits for Jen when Stacey wants to go out, is the prototype of all the characters in the novel: that is, she has a formidable façade, but a vulnerable psyche. Perfectly packaged, with fashionable clothes, flawless makeup, and elegant hairdo, Tess makes Stacey feel like a frump (9).

But there is no telling what goes on behind this polished veneer. Stacey thinks, "what can I do for her that would be any use? Let her pour out her woes? She never does. Maybe she hasn't got any, not really to speak of. I look at her, done up like a Christmas present, and I wonder what's actually inside. Maybe nothing. How can you tell unless people say?" (169–70).

But beneath this polished veneer, Tess is a deeply troubled personality. The first clue to her disturbance is her goldfish bowl, a gendered microcosm, where she watches the big fish eat the little fish — "Dog eat dog and fish eat fish" (92), Stacey reflects cynically. But the goldfish episode escalates when Katie discovers Tess forcing Jen to watch the male fish devour the female fish: *The little fish doesn't want to get eaten up but she's silly, isn't she? She doesn't run away and hide. So the big fish catches her, see? Watch now — look what he's doing to her. Nasty — he's nasty, isn't he?"* (191).

When Tess attempts suicide by swallowing sleeping pills, Jake and Stacey endeavour to reconstruct the sources of her death wish, realizing that they have failed to interpret the fatal clues correctly. The reader, however, has realized that Tess is vulnerable, even neurotic. Tess calls herself "highly strung" (202) and recalls her father saying, *"Tess, quit jumping around like a flea — you get on my nerves"* (202). Tess has an inferiority complex about her lack of sense of humour: her father said, *"Tess, when God gave out the sense of humor, he missed you"* (91). Stacey learns that slim hips don't bring happiness.

Stacey blames herself for not seeing beyond the surface: "Why didn't I? I always envied her for being so glamorous. I couldn't see anything else" (247). She blames herself for not trying to do anything: "I'm so damn sorry   I did know she was upset sometimes and I might have tried   but I didn't" (247).

Jake Fogler: Media Man

Tess's husband is a media man who reinforces the theme of communication: "Jake Fogler is a radio actor who is fond of talking about the breakdown of verbal communications and the problems of semantics in mass media" (78). Jake is embittered because his homely appearance relegates him to radio: "He has a talented voice, but he does not stand a look-in with TV" (78), because his "enormous glasses and slightly worn face give him the look of an aging owl-like boy caught in some moment of nefariousness" (84). Stacey is contemptuous of men "like Jake Fogler, about three feet tall with heavy-rimmed glasses and semi-collapsed chests, talking earnestly about media or some damn thing" (48).

But even Jake has a vulnerable interior, as Stacey discovers after Tess attempts suicide. Removing his glasses, because he has been crying, "He looks younger and less owlish" (246). His voice, usually confident, is full of "pain and bewilderment" (247). Ironically, "He was the one who used to tell me slickly that I had a death wish because I would have liked from time to time to be on a snow mountain by myself, no voices" (247), Stacey reflects. Now he blames himself, citing their childlessness as a reason for Tess's despair. He assumed Tess was confident because she was beautiful, whereas he looked like a chimpanzee (248).

Bertha and Julian Garvey: Minute Replica

Bertha and Julian Garvey are a minute replica of the reflection that the Foglers cast on the MacAindras. Bertha, as her name suggests, is a down-to-earth character. The initial description of her appearance is an excellent example of Laurence's ability to paint a complete personality with a few deft strokes: "Bertha comes into the living room. Pressing sixty, corseted to the point of shallow breathing, grey hair with slightly too true-blue rinse and done in a profusion of springy curls, hands big and capable — telling what her life work has been — eyes always a little worried behind upcurled green-framed glasses" (78).

But even earthy Bertha has her secret sorrows. One New Year's Eve she confessed to Stacey, "shedding absurd cartoon tears . . . into her Bloody Mary" (79), that, as the daughter of a high-rigger who lopped himself off along with the top of a Douglas fir, she swore never to marry a lumberman. Instead, she married Julian, a clerk in the camp: "*Julian was my fate, Stacey, but he can't forget I never went beyond grade school*" (79).

Julian Garvey is an unprepossessing little man: "He has a wispy tonsure of pepper-grey hair, and his seamed red mottled face resembles a surly gnome" (199). Street saint and house devil, Julian is "invariably courteous, even exaggeratedly so" with Stacey, but "saves his salvos for Bertha" (199). His bark is worse than his bite, however, because Julian's crotchety tones stem from his fear that Tess's suicide will give Bertha "fancy notions" (250).

Thus, the minor characters reflect the major figures, illuminating them.

THEMES: THE DYNAMICS OF DILEMMAS

In "Gadgetry or Growing," Margaret Laurence summarizes the complex nexus of connected themes that she has constructed in *The Fire-Dwellers*:

> I had, or felt I had, perhaps rather too many interlocking themes to deal with, but these were all inherent in Stacey and her situation, so no one thread could be abandoned without weakening the total structure, and yet, I was appalled at the number of threads. They may not seem too many to you, but to me at the time they seemed multitudinous — the relationship between a man and woman who have been married many years, when the woman does not have any real area of her life which is her own; the frustration of Stacey in trying to communicate with Mac and her ultimate realization of his bravery and his terrible hangups in having to deal with his problems totally alone; the relationship between generations — Stacey and Mac in relation to their children, as parents, and to their own parents as children; the sense of anguish and fear which Stacey feels in bringing up her kids in a world on fire; and also the question of a middle-aged woman having to accept middle-age and learn how to cope with the essential fact of life, which is that the process of life is irreversible. So — these themes. But how to express these things in Stacey's dilemma without saying them in so many words, without actually ever stating them? (87)

The Fire-Dwellers demonstrates a distinctive dynamic: all the themes, like the characters, are delineated in terms of conflicts — or dilemmas, to use Laurence's own term. The major thematic conflicts are between appearance and reality, identity and community, communication and integrity, life and death, and, perhaps more important still, negation and affirmation or damnation and salvation — other ways of viewing what Laurence has said in the passage above.

APPEARANCE VERSUS REALITY:
FACTS AND FICTIONS

Appearances: Masqueraders and Cave-Dwellers

Just as fictional fighting in westerns wars with real violence in Viet Nam on television, so appearance wars with reality in real life. Characters wear masks to hide their vulnerability, façades that appear strong on the surface. People employ clothing and makeup to mask their fragility, hide in caves of their own creation, and resort to hypocrisy, silence and lies to conceal their sentiments. Their double monikers signify their dual personalities — Stacey for Anastasia, Buckle for Arbuckle, Mac for Clifford MacAindra, and Thor Thorlakson for Vernon Winkler — because they conceal secret selves behind confident façades. As the layers peel away, we see that they are vulnerable beneath their veneers.

Tess Fogler, perfectly packaged with impeccable clothes, Queen Hatshepsut cosmetics and flawless coiffure, is the prototype for the characters. But Tess's thoughts remain a mystery behind her formidable façade, until she surprises with a suicide attempt. Stacey wonders "What cat noises go on in her head?" (9). She ruminates, "I look at her, done up like a Christmas present, and I wonder what's actually inside. Maybe nothing. How can you tell unless people say?" (169–70).

All the characters wear masks, whether they use makeup or not, recalling the dramatic masks of ancient Greek actors or the bear masks of Indian totems. Valentine Tonnerre, "expert at concealment" (241), paints a lipsticked cupid's bow over her real mouth, like a comic mask superimposed over a tragic one (239). Stacey recalls her own face "distorted into a swollen mask like the face of a woman drowned, the features blurred" (107). Recalling her father's death mask, Stacey reflects, "Perhaps it isn't that the masks have been put on, one for each year like the circles that tell the age of a tree. Perhaps they've been gradually peeled off, and what's there underneath is the face that's always been there for me, the unspeaking eyes, the mouth for whom words were too difficult" (157).

Characters employ clothing as camouflage. Stacey wears her hat and veil "as a disguise" (132), thinking, *"Under this chapeau lurks a mermaid, a whore, a tigress"* (15). She imagines she wears gloves to conceal her stigmata (101) and wishes for a kaftan to conceal her flesh when she makes love with Luke (187).

Characters also hide in caves: Stacey thinks, "I sometimes see us like moles, living in our underground burrows, with eyes that can't stand any light" (151).[9] Mac is a cave-dweller who has gone "underground, living in his own caves" (24); "he finds his exit" (30) where no one can follow. His study is a retreat, "where he can shut himself away, amid his business files and racing car magazines and Playboy" (60). But Stacey is a cave-dweller too. She wishes to bury herself in a snowy mountain cave (14). Luke exhorts, "Come out. From wherever you're hiding yourself" (167). Stacey reflects, *"If only I could get out.* What if everybody is thinking that, in some deep half-buried cave of themselves?" (231).

Jen is not the only character "determined not to communicate" (9). Mac uses silence as a screen, just as Buckle employs laughter "as both weapon and wall" (239). Hypocrisy is the most sophisticated façade, however, and Stacey is past-mistress of that art of concealment. Stacey's hypocrisy is illustrated by the division between what she says and what she thinks: "What goes on inside isn't ever the same as what goes on outside. It's a disease I've picked up somewhere" (34), she complains. "These lies will be the death of me" (34), she fears; but the question is, "How to stop telling lies?" (70). She prays, "God forgive me a poor spinner" (119), for "My kingdom it extendeth from lie to shining lie" (177). Stacey writes two letters home to her mother — the actual one recording decorous hypocrisies and an imaginary one revealing the unvarnished truth.

Reality: "Know Thyself"

The antidote to hypocrisy and mendacity is honesty. Before the characters can come out of their caves, however, they must achieve confidence in themselves. Before they can express themselves, they must first *know* themselves. Before they can empathize with others, they must understand them. Therefore, the issue of overcoming hypocrisy and mendacity and accepting reality involves the theme of identity and community.

Identity: *"Help, I'm Schizophrenic"*

The search for identity, particularly female identity, was a major subject for fiction throughout the sixties and seventies, especially feminist fiction. *The Fire-Dwellers* is in the forefront of this sub-genre, for Stacey embodies the dilemma of identity. Laurence shows how difficult it is for a person, especially a woman who is also a wife and mother, to maintain her sense of her self as a unified subject in the face of a culture which fragments the personality. Society constructs the female subject in conflicting roles that exclude the self. Somebody's wife, somebody's mother, somebody's daughter and somebody's sister, Stacey has forgotten who she is. She asks, "Who is this *you*?" and replies, "I don't know" (159). The problem occurs when "the woman does not have any real area of her life which is her own" ("GG" 87). Stacey voices her dilemma:

> Listen, God, I know it's a worthwhile job to bring up four kids. You don't need to propagandize me; I'm converted. But how is it I can feel as well that I'm spending my life in one unbroken series of trivialities? The kids don't belong to me. They belong to themselves. It would be nice to have something of my own, that's all. I can't go anywhere as myself. Only as Mac's wife or the kids' mother. (89–90)

The dilemma of the mother may be the major dilemma of the contemporary world, because it involves essential ethical and metaphysical questions. Stacey is caught on the horns of her (and every mother's) dilemma — whether to live for herself or sacrifice herself for her family.

Motherhood seems Stacey's only justification for existing. When she ponders the Day of Judgment, "God will say *Stacey MacAindra, what have you done with your life?* And I'll say, *Well, let's see, Sir, I think I loved my kids.* And He'll say, *Are you certain of that?* And I'll say, *God, I'm not certain about anything any more*" (14). She concludes, "They nourish me and yet they devour me, too" (20). Sometimes Stacey gets fed up and decides, "I'm bloody sick of trying to cope. I don't want to be a good wife and mother" (161).

Mothers have their identity trapped between generations. *The Fire-Dwellers* demonstrates "the relationship between generations — Stacey and Mac in relation to their children, as parents, and to their own parents as children" ("GG" 87). Significantly, the novel opens with Stacey rushing home to her children and ends with her awaiting the arrival of her sister and mother. The matriarch is caught in the middle: "I stand in relation to my life both as child and as parent, never quite finished with the old battles, never able to arbitrate properly the new, able to look both ways, but whichever way I look, God, it looks pretty confusing to me" (46). Two-faced like Janus, Stacey must turn the other cheek.[10]

Stacey's memories of her own youth portray her mother unsympathetically. But when Stacey compares her own problems with her husband and children with those of her mother, she gradually begins to see her mother sympathetically and to recognize that the parallels are ironically close: "She's had her troubles. As I know now" (277). Stacey even begins to sympathize with Katie as well.

But apart from her roles as wife and mother, sister and daughter, Stacey's sense of her self is shadowy. An invisible woman, she looks in the mirror "to make sure I'm really there" (132), for she appears to be doing a "disappearing act" (55). She thinks, "What's left of me? Where have I gone?" (70). She begins to doubt that she even exists, "now that I'm not seen" (138). She dreams she is carrying her own severed head, symbolizing the severance of her essence from her existence (115). She imagines God saying, *Sometimes I wonder if I even exist.* And I'd say, *I know what you mean, Lord. I have the same trouble with myself* (14).

Stacey cautions, "God, pay no attention. I'm nuts. I'm not myself" (156). Like her sister Rachel in *A Jest of God*, Stacey sometimes wonders if she is going crazy: "I'm a freak" (94), she fears. She thinks that if Mac knew what really went on in her mind, he would have her certified for insanity (57).

Stacey's identity is split like Rachel's: "Help, I'm schizophrenic" (106), she exclaims. Her schizoid condition is illustrated by dialogues like this one: "Who're you? One of your other selves" (106).

Stacey's dilemma of identity is signified by her names. *Stacey*, short for "Anastasia" (90), from the Latin word *stasis*, meaning stability, as in the *status quo*, is ironic, because Stacey is kinetic, not static, although she does provide stability for those around her. Caught between her past name, "Stacey Cameron," and her current label, "Mrs. C. MacAindra," she addresses herself by various epithets, from "dream girl" (170) to "female Saint" (231), from "clown" (122) to "doll" (13), from "Idiot child" (177) to "rotten old bitch" (9).

The encrustations of roles over her original self parallel the layers of fat smothering her slender sylph-like self-image. Stacey thinks, "I wanted to explain myself. I still do. Wait, you! Let me tell you. I'm not what I may appear to be. Or if I am, it's happened imperceptibly, like eating what the kids leave on their plates and discovering ten years later the solid roll of lard now oddly living there under your own skin. I didn't used to be. Once I was different" (70). She remembers "Stacey, traveling light, unfearful in the sun, swimming outward as though the sea were shallow and known, drinking without indignity, making spendthrift love in the days when flesh and love were indestructible" (70–71).

Stacey fights middle age, rejecting her wife-and-mother role, and struggles to resuscitate her youthful self. She knows her children think "I'm prehistoric, and it bugs me. I'm sorry, but it does. I'm not a good mother. I'm not a good wife. I don't want to be. I'm Stacey Cameron, and I still love to dance" (124). So Stacey dances to "Tommy Dorsey Boogie" (124), as she did in the Flamingo Dance Hall in Manawaka at seventeen. Not until she espies Katie dancing "simple and intricate as grass" does she sees herself truly: "Stacey MacAindra, thirty-nine, hips ass and face heavier than once, shamrock velvet pants, petunia-purple blouse, cheap gilt sandals high-heeled, prancing squirming jiggling" (127). She realizes, "The truth is that I haven't been Stacey Cameron for one hell of a long time now. Although in some ways I'll always be her, because that's how I started out. But from now on, the dancing goes on only in the head" (276).

Community: Surprised By Sympathy

Since her sense of identity is so fragile, Stacey feels threatened by other people, even her husband. Eventually she realizes that sympathy, not animosity, is the antidote to the poison of personal conflict: "Wouldn't it be strange if I could ever stop thinking in terms of *them* and *me*?" (189), she wonders.

The first time Stacey overcomes the barrier between herself and other people is when she is surprised by sympathy for Buckle

Fennick, a life-long adversary: "I never before in my life felt sorry for Buckle Fennick" (59). After his death, Stacey sheds tears for Buckle in a belated "requiem for a truck driver" (239).

Stacey's sympathy for Buckle extends to Mac when she realizes that Mac took Buckle on "for life" (219), after saving him from death. Stacey also recognizes Mac's "acceptance of the responsibilities he took on long ago when he never suspected what they might mean" (62) — responsibility for a growing family. Laurence remarks Stacey's "ultimate realization of his bravery and his terrible hangups in having to deal with his problems totally alone" ("GG" 87). Eventually Stacey realizes, "Mac has to pretend he's absolutely strong, and now I see he doesn't believe a word of it and never has. Yet he's a whole lot stronger than he thinks he is. Maybe they all are. Maybe even Duncan is. Maybe even I am" (260).

Eventually Stacey also begins to accept her responsibilities to her own community with good grace. When she invites her aging father-in-law to move in with them and realizes she will have to escort him to the bathroom, she thinks, "If you think it'll be awful for you, doll, how do you think he'll feel about it? Matthew, who doesn't even like to admit he has any natural functions" (256). When she learns from her sister's letter that Rachel and their aging mother are moving out to Vancouver, Stacey can be generous: "Rachel has had her all alone all these years. . . . it'll mean a lot to her to see the kids. I can't begrudge her. She's had her troubles. As I know now" (277).

FREEDOM VERSUS RESPONSIBILITY: "THE PROMISED LAND OF ONE'S OWN INNER FREEDOM"

Freedom: Escape Artist

Stacey's need to rediscover her true identity makes her want to escape from her roles as wife and mother. "I'm trapped" (194), she exclaims. Her home, "This fortress, which I'd like to believe strong" (18), becomes a prison holding her in, as well as a fort keeping others out: "My boundaries are four walls" (69).

Stacey's escape fantasies focus on the mountains and ocean around the city: "Sometimes I look through the living-room window at the snow mountains, far off, and I wish I could go there, just for a while, with no one else around and hardly any sounds at all, the wind muttering, maybe, and the snow in weird sculptures and caverns, quiet" (14). An escape artist, Stacey is also the original ladybird: whenever she leaves "Home Sweet Home" (104), she fears her house will burn down.

Stacey's escape fantasies involve lakes and rivers, rain forests and snowy mountains. Enter Luke Venturi, who offers to fulfil Stacey's escape fantasy by inviting her to accompany him up north to the Cariboo country (208). Stacey replays his proposal: "Luke. *I think I'll just hitch and see what happens. I'd like to go north. That's a great country, Stacey. Up the Skeena River — Kispiox, Kitwanga, crazy names like that. Northern jungle, rain forest —* " (263).

Many women, wives and mothers, did abandon their families in the sixties and seventies in order to find themselves — like Nora in Ibsen's *Doll's House*. Numerous novels, from Ethel Wilson's *Swamp Angel* (1954), through Doris Lessing's *A Proper Marriage* (1954), to Constance Beresford-Howe's *The Book of Eve* (1973), to name just a few, depicted women doing precisely that. Escaping responsibility was never the answer for Margaret Laurence, however.

Responsibility: Original Ladybird

Eventually, Stacey learns to accept her responsibilities and recognize her escape fantasies for what they are — adolescent daydreams. This is brought home to her brutally when she realizes that she is literally old enough to be Luke's mother. But Luke inspires Stacey to recognize her responsibilities when he asked her the essential question that men have been asking women ever since Chaucer's Loathly Lady — "What *do* you want?" Stacey, the original ladybird, replies, "I have to go home" (209) — Stacey's choice — prompting Luke to repeat the Ladybird nursery rhyme. Stacey's acceptance of her responsibilities is confirmed by the near-drowning of her favourite child, Duncan. Stacey reflects stoically:

The fun is over. It's been over for some time, only you didn't see it before. No — you saw it all right but you couldn't take it. You're nearly forty. You got four kids and a mortgage, and in just over three years Katie will be ready for university if she works hard enough, which is dubious. I guess the fun's been over

68

for Mac for quite a while. It would be nice if we were different people but we are not different people. We are ourselves and we are sure as hell not going to undergo some total transformation at this point. (263–64)

Stacey realizes, "I was wrong to think of the trap as the four walls. It's the world" (276). It is not just her home but the whole world that is on fire.

LIFE VERSUS DEATH: "SCARED TO DEATH OF LIFE"

Suicide: "Death Wish"

Stacey's escape fantasies are not limited to lakes and mountains, however. Sometimes she is tempted by the last trip — suicide. Her yearning for the snowy mountains is interpreted as a "death wish" (14). Even her escape fantasy about the Skeena River, where the ancient-eyed boatman ferries passengers across the turbulent waters, like a Charon figure ferrying dead souls across the River Styx to the underworld, expresses a death wish. Luke calls the land of ancient totems across the Skeena the land of "the living dead" (208). Concealing her father's old army revolver is a tangible symbol of suicide — the great escape.

Death is a central theme in all of Laurence's novels — understandably, since both her parents died when she was just a young child. Sylvia Fraser labels Laurence a "blood" child, suffering from "stigmata of the soul" (286).

The Fire-Dwellers is no exception: its pages are punctuated by deaths. The novel opens with the death of Peter Challoner in a car accident. When Ian is almost hit by a car as he runs out onto the street after a ball, just as Peter did, he is shaken. Stacey realizes that, unlike most young people, "Ian knows he's going to die" (197). Duncan is almost drowned at the seashore, and Buckle Fennick is killed when he plays Russian roulette on wheels once too often. Valentine Tonnerre tells Stacey that she is soon to take a "Long trip. The last one" (242), and Tess Fogler attempts suicide. Stacey's father, the alcoholic undertaker Niall Cameron, is the ghost who haunts *The Fire-Dwellers*, just as he does Laurence's sister novel, *A Jest of God*.

Life: "No Pre-mourning"

Stacey is sometimes tempted by suicide, the last trip: "sometimes I want to abdicate, only that. Quit. Can't" (131). Stacey stifles her suicidal impulses for the sake of her family: "I'm in forevermore, like it or not" (118). Laurence admires Stacey's "strong survival instincts" ("GG" 88), just as Stacey admired "such a simple knowledge of survival" (13) demonstrated by the hardy seagulls. As Laurence says, "her real self-discovery was that she was a survivor" (GGI 202).

After Tess's suicide attempt, Katie asks her mother hesitantly, "Don't ever pull that stunt like she did will you?" (249), and Mac asks Stacey significantly what she has done with her father's war revolver (279). In a gesture that recalls King Arthur's Excalibur or Ethel Wilson's Swamp Angel, Stacey has hurled the gun into Timber Lake, drowning death in a dramatic gesture that confirms a rejection of death and an affirmation of life.[11] Eventually, Stacey comes to agree with her instructor that *Pre-mourning is a form of self-indulgence* (15). Pinning up a sign saying *"No Pre-Mourning"* (253) on her refrigerator, Stacey elects life.

NEGATION VERSUS AFFIRMATION: "LET IT BE"

Negation: "Speak the Unspeakable"

Affirmation is more than mere survival, however. Living in the hell-fires of contemporary culture and frenetic family life has proven such a torment for Stacey that she considered suicide as an escape. The antidote to the pain is not to be found in the external dimension, however, but in the internal one. Stacey said, "I was wrong to think of the trap as the four walls. It's the world" (276). But *she* was wrong. The ultimate prison is the cell of the self. As Laurence says, we must find "the promised land of one's own inner freedom" ("TYS" 21). Only in the deep well of the spirit can one find the solution to the flames of hell fire.

Affirmation: "Accept the Unacceptable"

The important events in contemporary women's fiction are not actual incidents but rather a movement of the spirit from negation to affirmation. Stacey had become negative about everything — marriage, motherhood, and even life itself. She was ready to "speak the unspeakable" (272). But eventually, she learns to "accept the unacceptable" (255). More important, she learns to accept the realities of life. Luke urges, "Let it be" (210), echoing the Beatles' beatitude, and she does.[12] As Hagar marvels, "Each day, so worthless really, has a rarity for me lately. I could put it in a vase and admire it, like the first dandelions" (*SA* 5). Finally, Stacey falls asleep on the eve of a new decade of her life, praying, "Give me another forty years, Lord, and I may mutate into a matriarch" (281) — like Hagar.

DAMNATION AND SALVATION: "HELL OF A REVELATION"

Damnation: "Day of Judgement"

More important to Laurence than the literal physical conflict between life and death is the spiritual conflict between salvation and damnation. *The Fire-Dwellers* is an intensely religious novel, with God in a cameo role. As Stacey's only confidant, God is a good listener, because He has a non-speaking part. Stacey thinks, "God knows why I chat to you, God — it's not that I believe in you. Or I do and I don't, like echoes in my head. It's somebody to talk to" (63).

Stacey views the world in Manichean terms. *The Fire-Dwellers* is full of angels and devils. Stacey calls Jennifer "angel bud" (265) and Thor Thorlakson "angelman" (229). Stacey is bedeviled by Thor, a "bat-winged Mephistopheles" (44). When her "God of thunder" (244) is debunked by Valentine Tonnerre, Stacey thinks, "Aren't there any demons left in hell? How in hell can we live without them?" (245).

Stacey sees the world as an inferno, where people burn in hell fire. "Hell" is Stacey's favourite exclamation, or even "Thrice hell" (49). "Damn you" (199) and "Go to hell" take on "Sardonic implications" (62) in the context of the fire-dwellers. Even Stacey's swear words are religious, including "for heaven's sake" (86) and "Jesus lover of my soul" (35), while Mac takes the Lord's name in vain, exclaiming, "Good God" (274) and "for Christ's sake" (75).

Stacey is intensely superstitious. When Duncan nearly drowns, she uses "rune words, trinket charms to ward off the evil eye" (267). She bargains with God: "If it was anything I did, take it out on me, not on him — that's too much punishment for me" (267). She realizes, "Judgment. All the things I don't like to think I believe in. But at the severe moments, up they rise, the tomb birds, scaring the guts out of me with their vulture wings. Maybe it's as well to know they're there. Maybe knowing might help to keep them at least a little in their place. Or maybe not. I used to think about Buckle that he was as superstitious as a caveman. I didn't know then that I was too" (270).

The original sinner, Stacey fears "The Day of Judgment" (14): "I seem to believe in a day of judgment, just like all my Presbyterian forebears did" (241). She anticipates the end of the world: "What will happen when the horsemen of the Apocalypse ride through this town?" (55), she wonders. When her children are threatened, Stacey fears she is being punished for her sins. But when Mac gets a new job, Stacey feels "As though I'd been forgiven after all" (34).

Salvation: "Call Me Blessed"

Stacey has always expected a revelation, like Paul on the road to Damascus: "I used to think there would be a blinding flash of light some day, and then I would be wise and calm and would know how to cope with everything and my kids would rise up and call me blessed. Now I see that whatever I'm like, I'm pretty well stuck with it for life. Hell of a revelation that turned out to be" (272). Perhaps the great revelation never comes. All we get are little daily miracles. Laurence elaborates on "The theme of survival — not just physical survival, but the preservation of some human dignity and in the end some human warmth and ability to reach out and touch others" (*HS* 17). That is what saves Stacey.

COMMUNICATION VERSUS INTEGRITY: BREAKING THE SOUND BARRIER

Communication: "Words Alone are Certain Good"

"The problem of communication is central in Margaret Laurence's novels," writes G.D. Killam. Laurence herself states, "we must attempt to communicate, however imperfectly, if we are not to succumb to despair or madness" (*LDC* 124–25). In *Heart of a Stranger*, Laurence declares her faith in the Word:

> I have spent fifteen years of my life writing novels and other things. I have had, if any faith at all, a faith in the word. *In the beginning was the Word, and the Word was with God, and the Word was God.* The kind of belief that many writers have — the belief that if we are to make ourselves known to one another, if we are really to know the reality of another, we must communicate with what is almost the only means we have — human speech. There are other means of communication, I know, but they are limited because they are so personal and individual. We can make love; we can hold and comfort our children. Otherwise, we are stuck with words. We have to try to talk to one another, because this imperfect means is the only one we have. (203)

Communication is a central theme in *The Fire-Dwellers*, emphasized by the fact that Stacey's youngest child Jennifer, "The World's One and Only Nontalking Opera Star" (69), is "determined not to communicate" (9). The novel opens with Stacey "trying to teach Jen a few human words" (7), for "Words alone are certain good."[13] Language is the most important medium of communication for human beings, because language is the faculty that separates humans from the other animals.

The theme of communication also relates closely to the theme of identity, because we define ourselves by expressing ourselves. Critic Christl Verduyn says that *The Fire-Dwellers* suggests "a conjunction of language and identity" (138). Stacey thinks, "I want to tell" (131): "I'd like to talk to somebody. Somebody who wouldn't refuse really to look at me, whatever I was like" (252). But she is scared to speak: "No wonder I'm afraid of having an anaesthetic or undergoing hypnosis. What if I talked? I'm a freak" (94).

We also define our selves through our relations with other people. When our lines of communication break down, so does our sense of our own identity. Relationships rely on verbal communication. Stacey wonders what goes on in the minds of the people around her, from her family and her friends to the flower people of Vancouver: "What do I know of it? Only what I read in the papers. What do they think about? Impossible for me to know? What do they think about me?" (70). Of her friend Tess Fogler, Stacey reflects, "I wonder what's actually inside. Maybe nothing. How can you tell unless people say?" (169–70).

Like her creator, Stacey believes in communication: "I think we should discuss everything" (105). She believes that "Everybody should stop from time to time and explain what they mean. But none of us in this house do" (67). She thinks that if she could just explain herself, everything would be all right: "Katie? Listen. Just let me explain. I can explain everything. Sure, Explainer of the Year, that's me. How can I explain anything? How can I tell you what you should be doing? I don't know what I should be doing. But I think if I don't tell you, it'll look bad. If I could level with you, would we be further ahead? Do you really want to know what I'm like? I can't believe it" (47). Certain phrases recur throughout the novel like refrains: "talk to me" (130), "Let me explain" (170), "I don't know what to say" (264), "What do you want me to say", "What do you *mean*" (113), and "I can't say anything right" (60, 119).

Stacey cannot communicate with any of her children: "I can't get through the sound barrier" (203), she complains, as she contemplates "All your locked rooms" (198). The generation gap has become a canyon, epitomized by Stacey's relationship with Katie. A hangover from the jitterbugging generation of boogie-woogie (100), Stacey seems "*antediluvian*" (15) to Katie.

Stacey feels as if she is in a glass cubicle, cut off from the rest of the world — like the hairdryer at the beauty salon: "everything in front of her eyes is taking place in silence, as though she were observing it through some thick and isolating glass barrier or like TV with the voices turned off" (93) — like Sylvia Plath's bell jar.[14] When people do speak, they fail to communicate: "I'm surrounded by voices all the time but none of them seem to be saying anything, including mine. This gives me the feeling that we may all be one-dimensional" (77).

Just as Rachel's constant request is "Listen," so Stacey's continual refrain is "talk to me" (113), demonstrating the dialogue between the two sister novels. Stacey makes this plea to each member of her family in turn: "Mac, talk to me. Mac? Katie? Ian? Duncan?" (130). While Stacey thinks, "Katie — talk to me," Katie says, "Go away, can't you?" (113). When Stacey expresses sympathy over the death of Ian's friend Peter Challoner, Ian says, "Can't you just shut up about it?" (109). When Stacey says to Mac, "If we could just talk about everything," he replies, "Can't you just *leave me alone?*" (154). When Ian echoes Mac's words, saying, "*Can't you just leave me alone?*" (198), Stacey is devastated: "Ian. Mac's words. Ian, don't — I can't bear it. And you can't bear the way I try to know, the way I try to enter your locked room, can you?" (198). But one after another, they all reject her, saying "Go away" (113), "shut up" (109), or "*leave me alone*" (154), as one by one they lock themselves in the caves of their rooms.

Stacey's major communication gap is with her husband, who has escaped from frenetic family life into an underground cave inside his skull. Mac's study is like a cell "where he can shut himself away, amid his business files and racing car magazines and *Playboy*, away from the yammering of his wife and young" (60). "Whatever the game happens to be, it's a form of solitaire for Mac" (44).

Stacey pleads silently, "Mac — let me explain. Let me tell you how it's been with me. Can't we ever say anything to one another to make up for the lies, the trivialities, the tiredness we never knew about until it had taken up permanent residence inside our arteries?" (25). But all of their conversations sound like Theatre of the Absurd dialogues — full of hollow platitudes, empty inanities, and ludicrous misunderstandings that utterly fail to communicate — like this one:

Hi. You're late, Mac.
My God. Is that my fault? I had to finish up before I started home.
I didn't mean it that way.
Well, that's how it sounded to me.
I'm sorry. I only meant you're late and isn't that too bad. For *you*, for heaven's sake, I meant.
Okay, okay, it doesn't matter.
Doesn't matter! That you misunderstand every single word I utter.
Oh Stacey, for God's sake. I'm tired. Quit exaggerating.
Okay, so I'm exaggerating. It would just be nice if you knew what I meant. (25–26)

Katie parodies "You and Dad yakking away at each other — *Whatsmatter? Nothing's the matter. No need to talk to me in that tone of voice.* Man, not for me" (112).

Mac complains, "I can't say anything right" (119), while Stacey complains, "you misunderstand every single word I utter." She says, "It would just be nice if you knew what I meant," and thinks, "If I knew what you meant, as well. Oh Mac. Talk. Please" (26). But "The slightest effort at speech seems too much for him lately, too debilitating" (33). Stacey complains to Luke: "he doesn't talk any more hardly at all can you imagine what it's like to live in the same house with somebody who doesn't talk or who can't or else won't and I don't know which reason it could be." But Luke is not listening: "Stacey all at once recognizes the parallel lines which if they go on being parallel cannot ever meet" (181–82).

But Stacey has to learn to listen too: "I'm always wanting him to talk, and when he does, I'm absent. Sad defection of duty" (41). She says, "Katie, I'm sorry. I guess I didn't hear. I only heard what was pertinent to you or what I imagined to be pertinent to you. In the same way that I used to wonder if my mother ever really listened to what I'd been saying" (274). Sometimes it is difficult to listen, as when Mac tells Stacey about Buckle: "Stacey cannot say anything to enable him to speak, because she is afraid of what he will say," but she realizes, "if he doesn't say, it'll be the worst thing that ever happened to him" (216).

Other forms of communication are important between human beings besides speech: touch, for example, can be very telling. But the communication gap between Stacey and Mac is sexual as well as verbal. Mac avoids touching Stacey, and when he does have sex with her, he makes hate, not love: "in bed he makes hate with her, his hands clenched around her collarbones and on her throat until she is able to bring herself to speak the release. *It doesn't hurt*" (150).

Stacey has an impulse to confess: "*Mea culpa*. It must be wonderful to be a Catholic. Pour it all out. Somebody listens" (106). Since Stacey has no one else to talk to, she makes a confidant of a God she is not even sure she believes in: "God knows why I chat to you, God — it's not that I believe in you. Or I do and I don't, like echoes in my head. It's somebody to talk to. Is that all? I don't know. How would I like to be only an echo in somebody's head? Sorry, God. But then you're not dependent upon me, or let's hope not" (63).

God is a good listener because he never answers back: "You want to know something, God? Sometimes all I want to do is sit down quietly in a secluded corner and bawl my goddam eyes out. Okay, so you don't want to know. I'm telling you anyway" (195). God's unspoken commandments may represent Stacey's conscience, her internalization of the high moral standards of behaviour that she continually fails to live up to: she remonstrates, "Ease up on me, God, can't you?" (204). God is like "BIG BROTHER . . . WATCHING YOU."[15] Stacey cautions, "Don't listen in, God — this is none of your business" (125).

Stacey is also driven to talk to herself: the two parts in these internal dialogues seem to be Stacey's *ego* and *superego*, in Freudian terms, arguing what she wants to do versus what she knows she should do: "Don't *think* — I command you. You do, eh? Who're you? One of your other selves" (106). Sometimes Stacey's hectoring voice seems an internalization of her mother's prissy platitudes: when she wants a stiff drink and the voice suggests Ovaltine, she snaps, "Oh get lost, you" (128). Stacey gets impatient with her Jiminy Cricket character, exclaiming, "Bugger off, voice" (189). Alone, she reflects, "How good it feels, no voices. Except yours, Stacey. Well, that's my shadow. It won't be switched off until I die. I'm stuck with it, and I get bloody sick of it, I can tell you" (158–59).

Voice is one of the most often recurring words in the novel. Stacey recalls "the lunatic voices of the loons, witch birds out there in the night lake, or voices of dead shamans, mourning the departed Indian gods . . . the unhuman voices, the begone voices that cared nothing for lights or shelter or the known quality of home" (159). She remembers *"the blues of the night freight trains across snow deserts, the green beckoning voices"* (125). Stacey has nightmares in which she can hear her children's voices calling to her from the flames of a forest fire (31). At a Richalife party, "The babble and babel of voices go on, rising to crescendo, to cacophony" (231). Bliss for Stacey means "no voices" (158).

Laurence distinguishes each character in her cast by their distinctive voice or idiom. Stacey swears Buckle Fennick gets lines like *"Don't mind if I do"* from "old B-grade movies" (49), whereas Tess Fogler favours euphemisms like "let me freshen your drink," instead of "Let me give you another slug of this drug" (47). Tess refers to the "Little Girls' Room . . . making the john sound like a council hall for countless nymphets" (48). But Stacey reflects, "Katie is always saying how outdated my slang is. Gosh. Gee. Twerp. Heavenly days" (48).

Laurence emphasizes the power of words. Words, especially names, have runic power for Stacey, like magic charms. When Stacey thinks that Ian has died, "she is speaking the one mourning word. Ian Ian Ian" (211). And when Duncan appears to have drowned, Stacey screams, "*Duncan! You've got to be all right.* The words have been screamed, and although she does not hear her own voice, she is suddenly aware of the words' total lie. They are rune words, trinket charms to ward off the evil eye, and that is all. There is nothing she can do" (267). When Duncan recovers, thanks to Ian's action, Mac's three little words, "You did fine" (269), are like magic to Ian. "*Everything is all right*" is Stacey's mantra.

But words can let us down. When she tries to comfort Duncan, Stacey thinks, "What words? I haven't got any. It isn't mine he wants anyway. It's Mac's and Ian's, and those he won't get" (111). Sometimes words fail to communicate: there are "too few words that tell any of us a damn thing about any of the others" (194). Morag Gunn, heroine of *The Diviners*, thinks, "*I used to think words could do anything. Magic. Sorcery. Even miracle. But no, only occasionally*" (D 5).

Stacey equates community and communication, seeing social responsibility in verbal form: Matthew is "desperate to make talking sounds, someone else who'd have to be told everything is all right" (66). Sometimes Stacey wants to "speak the unspeakable" (272). With Valentine Tonnerre, however, she acknowledges "The necessary lie": "Too little can be said, because there is too much to say" (244). Eventually, Stacey begins to agree with Mac about the pointlessness of speech: "Why talk? Mac doesn't like to, and he's right. What good does it do?" (117), because "There isn't any use in talking. It doesn't change anything" (58).

Luke's attraction for Stacey is largely as a listener: "I can only break through [the sound barrier] with one person. Luke Luke Luke" (203). Stacey can confide in Luke because he is a stranger: once she has confided in him about the revolver, she can then confess to Mac. So Luke teaches Stacey to speak. She even catches herself echoing him: "*Hey, how about that?* is Luke's phrase" (195).

Luke becomes her Father Confessor, offering wine and inquiring, "What's the bad news?" (164). Luke does give Stacey faith — confidence in communication *and* in relationships. She thinks, "I'd like to start again, everything, all of life, start again with someone like you — with you — with everything simpler and clearer. No lies. No recriminations. No unmerry-go-round of pointless words" (189). She reflects, "I want to explain myself to him, make myself real to him. I want to say — look, this is what I'm like" (188). But Stacey realizes that Luke wants a confidante too, someone who will assure him that "*Everything's all right*" (185).

Luke helps Stacey to communicate in another important way, however. If not "tea and sympathy," he offers Stacey "coffee and sex" (206). He listens and loves, with no strings attached. Once she has made love with Luke, she is able to make love with Mac: "they make love after all, but gently, as though consoling one another for everything that neither of them can help nor alter" (279). If not "Epithalamium Twenty Years After" (49), it is nevertheless a reunion of sorts.

Integrity: "The Whole Truth and Nothing But The Truth"

Laurence believes that "human beings are capable of great communication and love and very often fall very far short of this. We simply do not communicate as much or at as deep a level as we are capable" (GGI 190). Laurence also declares:

> I feel that human beings ought to be able, *ought* to be able to communicate and touch each other far more than they do, and this human loneliness and isolation, which obviously occurs everywhere, seems to me to be part of man's tragedy. I'm sure one of the main themes in all my writings in [sic] this sense of man's isolation from his fellows and how almost unbearably tragic this is.... When I was very much younger I believed that total communication between two people was possible, but it isn't. At least I don't think it is. The great thing I suppose is to understand this and accept it. (DCI 105)

This is the lesson that Stacey must also learn. Just as Mac must learn to speak, Stacey must learn to respect his integrity as an individual and his right to privacy. After all, she does not really tell anyone, except God or her own alter ego, what she really thinks, because she realizes that the truth would be too destructive: "Why did I ever once feel that to tell the truth the whole truth and nothing but the truth would be a relief? It would be dynamite, that's all it would be. It would set the house on fire" (257).

Mendacity as well as secrecy protects personal privacy. Stacey resorts to lies as well as hypocrisy to preserve her integrity. She becomes so addicted to "habitual fib-telling" (63) that she is trapped in her own fabrications: "How to stop telling lies?" (70). "These lies will be the death of me sooner than later, if they haven't already been" (34), she fears. "I say I am not much in love with the lies, but they don't get less — they get more. How can this be? God forgive me a poor spinner" (119), for "My kingdom it extendeth from lie to shining lie" (177).

Initially, Stacey is disturbed by "The silences" (44) between herself and Mac, echoing the "tomb silences" (27) between her parents. Eventually Stacey appreciates the importance of silence in protecting the individual's integrity. When she realizes there is no point upsetting Mac by telling him that he's been scared by a straw man whose real name is not Thor Thorlakson but Vernon Winkler, she reflects, "It's not actually like lying. It's just refraining from saying. The silences aren't all bad. How do I know how many times Mac has protected me by not saying? He probably noticed the burn on my hand that time" (264).

When Mac speaks those three little magic words to Ian, "You did fine" — like Mr Ramsay's cryptic "Well done" to his son James in Virginia Woolf's 1927 novel, *To the Lighthouse*[16] — Stacey acknowledges the masculine mode of minimalism:

— That's the most Mac will ever be able to say. They're not like me, either of them. They don't want to say it in full technicolor and intense detail. And that's okay, I guess. Ian gets the message. It's his language, too. I wish it were mine. All I can do is accept that it is a language, and that it works, at least sometimes. And maybe it's mine more than I like to admit. Whatever I think that I think of it, it's the one I most use. (269–70)

Stacey learns to respect others' integrity: "Stacey wants to touch [Katie], to hold fast to her and at the same time to support her. But she expresses none of these, having to be careful, unable to gauge accurately, having to guess only" (253).

Stacey must learn there are other forms of expression besides words. Crying is a critical kind of communication, revealing the human vulnerability beneath the veneer. When Bertha Garvey sheds cartoon tears into her Bloody Mary (79) or when Jake Fogler weeps over his wife's suicide attempt (246), each is humanized. Each member of the MacAindra family weeps, illustrating their vulnerability and initiating communication. As a woman, Stacey weeps most easily and often: when she sees the boy hit by the car (16), when she sings a hymn (69), when Matthew repeats the Psalm (152), when Luke tells the story about the mother who took off (165), when Tess attempts suicide (249) and when Duncan almost drowns (268).

Weeping is an issue in the MacAindra household, because Mac, as the strong silent type, believes that real men don't cry, and he attempts to condition his sons into the stiff-upper-lip macho mould. When Duncan cries after hurting his hand, Mac goes straight into his sergeant-major routine (110).

But crying is proof of life: when Duncan is given the breath of life by a young lifeguard after he almost drowns, "he begins to cry, the attenuated wail of a very young child, an infant voice" (268), signalling his survival. When Ian, who is made in the same stiff-upper-lip mould as Mac, weeps over the death of his friend and his own narrow escape, Stacey realizes that he has understood the fact of death: "Ian cried. Ian. Who never cries" (197). Katie cries when her mother forbids her to attend an Adult film, although she is disconcerted when she discovers Stacey weeping over Tess Fogler's suicide attempt: "please just don't cry Mum *please*" (249), because children are disturbed by proof of their parents' vulnerability. When Luke gives Stacey the right to weep, he begins her healing process, assuring her that real women can cry. When Mac finally breaks down after identifying Buckle's broken body, it is like a bursting dam: "He is crying now, the lung-wrenching spasms of a man to whom crying is forbidden" (216). Afterward, Mac can speak to Stacey, expressing his feelings. Stacey sheds belated tears for Buckle too in a "requiem for a truck driver" (239).

Stacey learns that there are other forms of communication besides speech. As Laurence says, "We can make love; we can hold and comfort our children" (*HS* 203). Looks can be very telling, and couples can communicate with a glance: "Stacey's jaw clamps shut as her brain receives the signal from Mac's red-flare-sending eyes" (40). Touching is important too, and Laurence makes eloquent use of hands. After Stacey has violently flung both boys to the floor, prompting Duncan's nightmare, Ian uncharacteristically reaches out a hand to her (29). When Stacey is worried, Duncan puts his hand in hers to reassure her (223).

After Buckle is killed, Mac holds Stacey: "Mac, who never touches her in public in case somebody might see, suddenly puts his arms around her again and holds her cruelly tight, blind to the streetlights, blind to Bluejay Crescent, holding her not for her need now but for his own" (213). Once he has admitted his need, Mac can even make love: "She moves towards him and he holds her" (279).

When it comes to the crunch, the children can express confidence in their mother's ability to communicate. Stacey thinks she never knows what to say, but Duncan is confident that "you'll think of something" (223). After Tess has forced Jen to watch one goldfish kill another, Katie says, "you would've known what to say. You always do. I never do" (192). Breaking the sound barrier is celebrated when Jen turns to her mother near the end of the novel and asks casually, "Want tea, Mum?" (273). Maybe the communication gap is bridgeable after all. Laurence emphasizes the theme of communication through the unique typography employed in *The Fire-Dwellers*, as we will see in the subsequent section on narrative method.

NARRATIVE METHOD: "VOICES AND PICTURES"

Laurence writes of *The Fire-Dwellers*, "What I want to get is the effect of voices and pictures — just voices and pictures" — another way of saying "audio-visual" ("GG" 87–88). Let us consider first "voices" and then "pictures."

Ventriloquism of Voices

Laurence declares, "The treatment of time and the handling of the narrative voice — these two things are of paramount importance to me in the writing of fiction." Therefore "it is so desperately important to discover the true narrative voice" ("TNV" 156–57). Laurence's most striking innovation in *The Fire-Dwellers* is her combination of first- and third-person narrative voices.

The Fire-Dwellers is the first and only one of Laurence's Manawaka novels to employ the omniscient third person, rather than the purely confessional first person. Laurence included the third person in *The Fire-Dwellers* because she is concerned to convey context as well as character, the fire as well as the dweller, to present the central character reacting to her cultural context. She explains, "I decided that a certain amount of external narration was necessary, partly to avoid the awkwardness of forward-moving which had plagued *A Jest of God*, and partly to give some distance to the reader's view of Stacey, for she was not the shut-in and withdrawn person that Rachel was" ("GG" 88).

Stacey's is still the central consciousness in *The Fire-Dwellers*, however, and her viewpoint and voice do dominate the narrative. Laurence explains:

Most of the fiction I have written in recent years has been written in the first person, with the main character assuming the narrative voice. Even when I have written in the third person, as I did in part of my novel *The Fire-Dwellers*, it is really a first-person narrative which happens to be written in the third person, for the narrative voice even here is essentially that of the main character, and the writer does not enter in as commentator. ("TNV" 156–57)

Although Stacey is not the official narrator of her own story that Rachel is in *A Jest of God* or Hagar in *The Stone Angel* or Morag in *The Diviners*, Stacey's character does dominate the narrative of *The Fire-Dwellers* nevertheless because Laurence believes that character dictates form. Laurence explains that "Form, in writing, concerns me more than it once did, but only as a means of conveying the characters and their particular dilemmas, because this matter of dealing with individual dilemmas seems to be my fate in writing" ("GG" 89).

In *The Fire-Dwellers*, Laurence develops an innovative narrative technique that succeeds in conveying both the internal subjective world of the character's thoughts and feelings and the external objective world of contemporary culture through alternating first- and third-person narrative methods. Laurence explains, "I did not want to write a novel entirely in the first person, but I did not want to write one entirely in the third person, either. The inner and outer aspects of Stacey's life were so much at variance that it was essential to have her inner commentary in order to point up the frequent contrast between what she was thinking and what she was saying" ("GG" 86). As Stacey exclaims, "What goes on inside isn't ever the same as what goes on outside" (34), and it is always a shock to be transported "Out of the inner and into the outer" (161).

In order to convey this schizophrenic state, Laurence embeds Stacey's stream-of-consciousness first-person narrative in an omniscient third-person narrative frame, alternating between internal and external dimensions. Each of Stacey's actual utterances is contradicted by a tacit commentary introduced by a subtle dash. When she invites Buckle Fennick to stay for dinner and he replies, "Twist my arm," she thinks rudely, "Will I, hell. Your arm needs less twisting than anybody's I know, you cheap bastard," but she says politely, "Sure, do stay. There's plenty. Let me get you a drink" (49). So hypocrisy triumphs over truth.

Internal Monologues: "Stacey's Voice"

Stacey's internal monologues, like the hero's soliloquies in a Shakespearean tragedy, are the heart of The Fire-Dwellers, conveying the major themes of the novel, as well as the central character's consciousness. Laurence emphasizes, "The inner monologue, of course, is strictly in Stacey's voice, and it was through this, largely, that I hoped to convey her basic toughness of character, her ability to laugh at herself, her strong survival instincts" ("GG" 88).

Certainly, Stacey's own voice, which Laurence calls "my own idiom, the ways of speech and memory of my generation" ("TYS" 22), leaves its stamp on the style of the novel. Stacey's vivid vernacular, with its colorful colloquialisms, dated slang and salty swear words, brands the narrative with Stacey's special stamp. Stacey's poetic imagination also distinguishes the style of The Fire-Dwellers.

Laurence's use of stream-of-consciousness technique takes us right inside Stacey's mind, as this impressionistic underwater reverie illustrates:

Everything drifts. Everything is slowly swirling, philosophies tangled with the grocery lists, unreal-real anxieties like rose thorns waiting to tear the uncertain flesh, nonentities of thoughts

floating like plankton, green and orange particles, seaweed—lots
of that, dark purple and waving, sharks with fins like cutlasses,
herself held underwater by her hair, snared around auburn-
rusted anchor chains (34)

Stacey's magic-carpet imaginings when inebriated are unpunctuated
and literally spaced out, like her free-associating, spaced-out state of
mind:

She is lying on a magic carpet. Must be a magic carpet, what else?
It is moving very rapidly, in upward and downward swooshes.
Each swirl leaves a color in its path   jet-trails of color smoke
one for each day of the week   pink   purple   peacock   blue
tangerine   green leaves   greensleeves   bird-feather   yellow
raspberry   no not raspberry   that's an essence   the essence of the
whole matter is is is (104)

So Stacey's impressionistic stream-of-consciousness monologues
contribute to the poetic undercurrents of Laurence's narrative.

REMINISCENCE: "CONNED INTO MEMORY"

Stacey's stream of consciousness flows forward into the future and
backward into the past, like Morag's river in *The Diviners*. The past
is ever-present for Laurence's characters, and Stacey counterpoints
past and present in a series of memories indicated by indentation.
Stacey's free-associating causes incidents in her present to trigger
remembrance of things past, as she is continually "Conned into
memory" (72). Laurence incorporates Stacey's history through over
forty of Stacey's memories, ranging from her childhood, through her
first love affair, to her honeymoon and the conception and birth of
her children. Through reminiscences like this one of her lost youth,
Stacey tries to come to terms with the process of middle-aging, the
ineluctable modality of the mortal: "Stacey, traveling light, unfearful
in the sun, swimming outward as though the sea were shallow and
known, drinking without indignity, making spendthrift love in the
days when flesh and love were indestructible" (70–71). Reminiscence

becomes psychoanalysis, as Stacey attempts to lay the ghosts of her past, recognizing that her heritage from her parents' past will be her legacy for her children's future.

FEMALE FANTASIES: DAYDREAMS AND NIGHTMARES

Just as important as Stacey's memories of the past are her fantasies of the future. Stacey copes with the disappointments of the quotidian by daydreaming, trying on destinies like dresses, as everybody does. Daydreams are delineated by italics to distinguish them from actuality. Stacey has nearly two dozen fantasies in all, but none of them can be more farfetched or more poignant than this one: *"Out there in unknown houses are people who live without lies, and who touch each other. One day she will discover them, pierce through to them. Then everything will be all right, and she will live in the light of the morning"* (85).

Several of Stacey's fantasies have significant connections with reality. For example, after wondering who she really is, she dreams that she is carrying her own severed head through a forest, symbol of her loss of identity (115). Sexually frustrated in her marriage, some of Stacey's daydreams are sex fantasies starring fictional figures (83, 94) or real people like Buckle Fennick (141).

Some of Stacey's fantasies are attempts to imagine the inner reality of members of her family. She imagines Mac's life on the road (22) or during his boyhood (121). She envisions the future of her children, as she imagines Ian's potential personae at nineteen (118). She tries out possible futures for herself, imagining herself as an architect's woman Friday (139).

Many of Stacey's dreams are actually nightmares where she is trapped in her fear of fire. Stacey, the original Ladybird, envisions a house fire threatening her family (141) or a forest fire from which she must save her four children (31). She imagines escaping from a possible holocaust by driving north into Cariboo country (160), or running away from the flames of life with Luke by crossing the river of reality with a ghostly ferryman to the never-never land of totems (222).

Many of Stacey's monologues are actually dialogues that she holds
with God, the closest she comes to prayer. Lacking any living mortal
in the tangible world that she can tell her troubles to, she pours out
her fears and frustrations to a God she is not even sure she believes
in:

> God knows why I chat to you, God — it's not that I believe in
> you. Or I do and I don't, like echoes in my head. It's somebody
> to talk to. Is that all? I don't know. How would I like to be only
> an echo in somebody's head? Sorry, God. But then you're not
> dependent upon me, or let's hope not. (63)

Stacey's conversations with God are like a dialogue with her superego, with God as the voice of conscience, a Jiminy Cricket character
looking over her shoulder and judging the moral rectitude of her
actions from the traditional standpoint of patriarchal society. Stacey
remonstrates, "Ease up on me, God, can't you?" (204). God is like
"BIG BROTHER . . . WATCHING YOU": she cautions, "Don't listen in,
God — this is none of your business" (125). Stacey demands a
feminist perspective: "God, don't talk to me like that. You have no
right. *You* try bringing up four kids" (156). She adds, "God, pay no
attention. I'm nuts. I'm not myself" (156).

Stacey holds internal dialogues with herself, arguments between
her desires and her ideals: "Don't *think* — I command you. You do,
eh? Who're you? One of your other selves. Help, I'm schizophrenic"
(106). She addresses herself in various voices, from her "placating
voice" (55) and her "loud harridan voice" (104) to her "good-wife-
and-mother voice" (49). *Voice* is one of the most often repeated
words in this novel. Stacey becomes impatient with her Jiminy
Cricket character, exclaiming, "Bugger off, voice" (189). Bliss for
Stacey means "no voices. Except yours, Stacey. Well, that's my
shadow. It won't be switched off until I die. I'm stuck with it, and I
get bloody sick of it, I can tell you" (158–59).

Laurence alternates Stacey's imagined dialogues with actual dialogue. *The Fire-Dwellers* is intensely dramatic: it almost reads like
the script of a play, composed largely of actual speeches, complete
with stage directions providing sound effects. Laurence conveys

conversation naturally, the way it really occurs in families with everyone speaking at once, interrupting each other, leaving sentences unfinished. This breakfast conversation, framed by radio announcements and punctuated by telephone rings, is a perfect example of her realistic dialogue:

THIS IS THE EIGHT-O'CLOCK NEWS BOMBING RAIDS LAST NIGHT
DESTROYED FOUR VILLAGES IN
    Mum! Where's my social studies scribbler?
    I don't know, Ian. Have you looked for it?
    It's gone. I gotta take it to school this morning
    Well, *look*. Katie, have you seen Ian's social studies scribbler?
    No, and I'm not looking for it, either. If he wasn't so
    Stacey, the party starts at eight tonight. Be ready, eh?
    Sure, yes yes of course. Duncan, eat your cereal.
    I hate this kind. Why do you always buy it?
    You say that about every kind I buy. C'mon. . . .
ROAD DEATHS UP TEN PER CENT MAKING THIS MONTH THE WORST
IN (86–87)

Laurence moves back and forth through time and space — from memories of the past to fantasies of the future, from internal monologue to external dialogue — through the technique of *montage*, where the narrative moves from scene to scene in a series of vignettes juxtaposed without any signposts to direct the reader. But Laurence does employ a skilful system of typography to signal to the alert reader which time frame we are in — whether past, present, or future — and which dimension we are in — whether quotidian actuality or remote mind-tripping.

TYPOGRAPHY OF PICTURES:
"SHORT SHARP VISUAL IMAGES"

The most significant aspect of *The Fire-Dwellers* may be its narrative form, especially the innovative use Laurence makes of typography, the presentation of print on the page. Laurence emphasizes her experimentation with narrative form: "the shape of this novel worried me very much before I began writing it, and I looked at and discarded many methods before I finally worked out the one in which the novel is written" ("GG" 86).

Ideally, Laurence wanted a multi-media form that would convey the frenetic multi-faceted quality of contemporary culture. In the sixties, art, especially film, was experimenting with multiple perspectives. Canada's first World's Fair, Expo 67 in Montreal, featured multiple film screens reflecting numerous images, like the multi-faceted eyes of a housefly. Laurence explains her plans: "I then thought the novel should be written in three or four columns, newspaper style, with three or four things happening simultaneously. Luckily, it occurred to me in time that few readers were likely to have three or four pairs of eyes" ("GG" 87).

Laurence believes that her narrative form was influenced by mass media:

Finally the form and material sorted themselves out. I was, I think, considerably influenced, although subconsciously, by years of TV watching. I kept thinking, "What I want to get is the effect of voices and pictures — just voices and pictures". I became obsessed with this notion, as it seemed to convey the quality of the lives I wanted to try to get across. It was only much later that I realized that "voices and pictures" is only another — and to my mind, better — way of saying "audio-visual". . . . I wanted the pictures — that is, the descriptions — whether in outer life or dreams or memories, to be as sharp and instantaneous as possible, and always brief, because it seemed to me that this is the way — or at least one way — life is perceived, in short sharp visual images which leap away from us even as we look at them. ("GG" 87–88)

Laurence emphasizes the need for simultaneity to recreate the confusion of contemporary culture: "The main need was for some kind of form which would convey the sense of everything happening all at once, simultaneously" ("GG" 86). Stacey complains, "It's the confusion that bothers me. Everything happens all at once" (18). Laurence's solution was to interweave multiple threads in a complex of fragments, like the pieces of a puzzle, connected by montage: "Narration, dreams, memories, inner running commentary — all had to be brief, even fragmented, to convey the jangled quality of Stacey's life" ("GG" 86).

Simultaneity raises the problem of selectivity, however. Laurence explains, "Obviously, if you are trying to get across the vast number of things which impinge upon the individual consciousness every minute of the day, you must be very selective and hope to convey quite a lot by implication rather than quantitative description. Either that, or write a novel of fifty thousand pages, which was very far from being my aim" ("GG" 86).

Laurence developed a telegraphic style in order to recreate this reality economically: "I wanted to write something in a kind of prose which would be much more spare and pared down than anything I had ever done before" ("GG" 86).

> With this last novel (which interests me more than the others, because I've just finished it and am not yet disconnected) the writing is more pared-down than anything I've written yet, but the form itself is (or so I believe) wider, including as it does a certain amount of third-person narration as well as Stacey's idiomatic inner running commentary and her somewhat less idiomatic fantasies, dreams, memories. ("TYS" 22)

Laurence's narrative form in *The Fire-Dwellers* is a postmodern potpourri reflecting the frantic quality of Stacey's world. In order to recreate this kaleidoscopic panorama of frenetic contemporary life with vivid verisimilitude, Laurence evolved a complex and innovative method of structuring her narrative by means of clever use of typography as signposts to guide the reader. Allan Bevan summarizes her methods succinctly in his 1973 Introduction to *The Fire-Dwellers*:

> Margaret Laurence, in this novel, uses a variety of narrative methods, although Stacey is always at the centre: Stacey's thoughts (introduced by a dash), her memories (indented on the page), her fantasies often in the form of SF words (in italics), the news from radio or the EVER-OPEN EYE (in capital letters), the narrator's comments more or less over Stacey's shoulder (in ordinary type and without dashes or italics), and conversations (again without introductory marks). (206)

Laurence introduces Stacey's monologues with a dash to contrast her private thoughts with her public speech. After she politely invites her father-in-law to accompany the family to the beach, for example, she thinks, "—Madwoman" (66).

Laurence indents Stacey's memories to distinguish them from present reality:

> Her memories were set to one side on the page in an attempt to clarify the fact that these are flashing in and out of her mind while she is doing other things. Incidentally, when I complained to one of Macmillan's sales' staff in England about the high price of *The Fire-Dwellers*, he said, "Well, Margaret, if you insist on wasting all that space on every page, what can you expect?" ("GG" 88)

Laurence explains her use of italics to distinguish Stacey's fantasies:

> The dreams and fantasies were put in italics only in order to identify them as dreams and fantasies, and also, perhaps, to provide a kind of visual variety on the page — something I have myself felt a need for, sometimes, in reading novels — that no one tone should go on too long, that there should be some visual break — and I think that probably our need for this kind of variety has been conditioned by films and TV. ("GG" 88–89)

Laurence chose to omit quotation marks around speech, to avoid conventional signposts of "he said" or "she said" and even to omit concluding punctuation at the end of sentences in order to make her dialogue realistic and dramatic:

> The reason that I did not use any quotation marks in *The Fire-Dwellers* for characters' speech to one another was that I wanted to get, once again, the sense of everything happening all at once, the way in which talk flows in and out of people's lives and is not cut off or separate from events. The reason that some sentences in Stacey and Mac's talk are unfinished or simply trail off is because that is the way they talked and, in fact, the way many people talk. ("GG" 89)

Laurence uses all capitals to convey radio newscasts and "The Ever-Open Eye" (57) of television, recreating the insistent blare of contemporary news media as they demand entrance into our domestic world and impinge on our personal lives:

EVER-OPEN EYE   A HILLSIDE AND SMALL TREES SEEN FROM HIGH
AND FARAWAY. THE SMOKE RISING IN ROLLING CLOUDS. VOICE:
ACCELERATED BOMBING IN THE AREA OF (116)

Laurence employs italics to reprint the numerous songs and hymns
that Stacey sings, and the numerous lines from literature, mythology
and the Bible that she quotes, such as, *"Save me, O God, for the
waters are come in unto my soul"* (152).

Laurence begins "Gadgetry or Growing: Form and Voice in the
Novel" thus:

> With the occasional rare genius — and let us never forget that
> great writers are exceedingly rare — the old forms are broken;
> truly new forms are evolved, and — as was the case, I believe,
> with James Joyce — the face of the language is changed. With
> the rest of us, the evolution of form is never totally new and is
> usually much less experimental or original than we might like to
> imagine, but it is an attempt at something new to us, an effort to
> discover a means — a vehicle, if you like — which is capable of
> getting across some of the things we feel compelled to try to
> communicate. (80)

Laurence modestly hopes that "I may discover what I'm looking for,
which — as far as form in writing is concerned — is the kind of vehicle
or vessel capable of risking that peculiar voyage of exploration which
constitutes a novel" ("GG" 89). There is no doubt about Laurence's
artistic success in creating a new narrative form for *The Fire-Dwellers*
that recreates contemporary culture colourfully.

STRUCTURE: "THE TREATMENT OF TIME"

Laurence begins her essay on "Time and the Narrative Voice" by
declaring:

> The treatment of time and the handling of the narrative voice —
> these two things are of paramount importance to me in the
> writing of fiction. Oddly enough, although they might seem to
> be two quite separate aspects of technique, in fact they are
> inextricably bound together. When I say "time," I don't mean

clock-time, in this context, nor do I mean any kind of absolute time — which I don't believe to exist, in any event. I mean historical time, variable and fluctuating. ("TNV" 156)

The treatment of time is indeed closely connected to the "narrative voice" which we considered in the previous section. Laurence elaborates on her view of time:

In any work of fiction, the span of time present in the story is not only as long as the time-span of every character's life and memory; it also represents everything acquired and passed on in a kind of memory-heritage from one generation to another. The time which is present in any story, therefore, must — by implication at least — include not only the totality of the characters' lives but also the inherited time of perhaps two or even three past generations, in terms of parents' and grandparents' recollections, and the much much longer past which has become legend, the past of a collective cultural memory. ("TNV" 156)

Laurence explains that the central character dictates the treatment of time:

Once the narrative voice is truly established — that is, once the writer has listened, really listened, to the speech and idiom and outlook of the character — it is then not the writer but the character who, by some process of transferal [sic], bears the responsibility for the treatment of time within the work. It is the character who chooses which parts of the personal past, the family past and the ancestral past have to be revealed in order for the present to be realized and the future to happen. This is not a morbid dwelling on the past on the part of the writer or the character. It is, rather, an expression of the feeling which I strongly hold about time — that the past and the future are both always present, *present* in both senses of the word, always now and always here with us. It is only through the individual presence of the characters that the writer can hope to convey even a fragment of this sense of time, and this is one reason, among others, why it is so desperately important to discover the true narrative voice — which really means knowing the characters so well that one can take on their past, their thoughts, their responses, can in effect for awhile *become* them. ("TNV" 157)

Time is critical for Stacey: thirty-nine years old at the outset, she stands on the brink of middle age, as the novel ends on the eve of her fortieth birthday.

FRAMEWORKS: FRAMED BY FIRE

Laurence structures time skilfully in *The Fire-Dwellers* through the use of framing devices. The novel begins and ends with the same tableau, with Stacey alone in her room confronting the reflection of her present self framed by the mirror, next to the framed photograph of her past self: "The full-length mirror is on the bedroom door. Stacey sees images reflected there, distanced by the glass like humans on TV, less real than real and yet more sharply focused because isolated and limited by a frame" (7). Stacey reflects, "*Is* time? How?" (15).

The opening and concluding passages are so similar (even the bedside books, His and Hers, remain unread) that one might think nothing had happened in between. But actually the descriptions of identical tableaux at the beginning and end of the novel frame a period crammed with crises. The action of Laurence's novels, however, and of most contemporary women's fiction, is subordinate to the real development — the "change of heart" (221). Through the moral development or spiritual growth required to surmount these current crises, the character discovers the strength to bury the past and face the future with affirmation.

Laurence reinforces this sense of immediacy by using further framing in her introduction. The first chapter begins with Stacey dressing for the day and ends with Stacey submerging into sleep — only to be awakened from her forest fire nightmare the next morning by her alarm clock: "Bloody morning once again" (31). Life, like Sisyphus' boulder, is something that must be faced anew every day.

Stacey's typical day presented in this first chapter is further framed by fire, beginning with the nursery rhyme about the ladybird flying home to her burning house and crying children, and finishing with

94

her forest fire fantasy, from which Stacey, the original ladybird, must rescue her offspring.

The framework — the opening scene portraying Stacey preparing to face a new day and the concluding scene presenting Stacey retiring at the end of the last day — suggests that the entire narrative has taken place over just one day — an effect Virginia Woolf achieves in her 1927 novel *To the Lighthouse*. These structuring devices actually frame a season, however, focusing on the summer vacation when Stacey's children are home from school and her period of peace and quiet is fractured — just like Stacey's sister's novel, *A Jest of God*. *The Fire-Dwellers* concludes, after Duncan's near-drowning at the seashore, with Stacey's children's return to school in the fall, as survival is assured and normality is reestablished: "September, and the kids go back to school" (272). So the rise and fall of the seasons parallel the rise and fall in the tides of men — or at least in the fortunes of the MacAindra family. That summer season constitutes a critical turning-point in Stacey's spiritual development, when her love affair inspires her "change of heart" (221) — just as Rachel's summer romance does.

Laurence also uses her theme song, the ladybird nursery rhyme, as a framing device, for it appears three times throughout the novel — at the beginning (7), the middle (209), and the end (280) — structuring the entire narrative. The rhyme relates to the title image of the fire-dwellers, Sandburg's epigraph about Nero fiddling in a world on fire, and all the fire imagery throughout the novel. The figurative level of imagery also structures the novel, symbolizing the profound themes that underlie the vivid verisimilitude of the surface action.

Laurence also employs letters to frame and structure the narrative. Stacey writes two letters home to her mother at a critical turning-point in her life — the real letter telling a facile falsehood and an imaginary epistle telling the unvarnished truth — delineating the two levels of the narrative, literal and figurative. Stacey's letter is answered at the end of the novel by her sister Rachel's missive announcing her imminent arrival, accompanying their aged mother. The pairs of letters also link the two sister novels together.

Stacey, like Laurence, is fascinated by the "mystery of the very concepts of *past, present and future*" ("TNV" 159), and she interweaves past and future with present through flashbacks and flashforwards.

FLASHBACKS: "FRAGMENTS FROM THE PAST"

Laurence structures past, present, and future very skilfully. In *The Stone Angel*, Hagar is "rampant with memory" (5). Her memories complete her history for the reader in a series of flashbacks arranged in chronological order leading up to the point of her death, as her whole life appears to flash before her eyes. In *The Fire-Dwellers*, Laurence employs a similar system of flashbacks through memory. But Stacey's memories are random, rather than chronological, to capture the frenetic quality of her life and her frantic state of mind. Laurence writes, "Stacey's memories are not flashbacks, nor do they occur in any chronological order. They are snatches, fragments from the past, because this seemed to me to be the way my own memories returned, and it appeared to me that the same would be true of Stacey, whose life is busy, and indeed often frantic" ("GG" 88).

The past is ever-present for Laurence: "For me the past is extremely real" (GGI 204). As Stacey observes, "The past doesn't seem even to be over" (235). She believes in "the sins of my fathers," for "debts are inherited" (241). Reminiscence becomes psychoanalysis, as Stacey lays the ghosts of her past, for her heritage from her parents' past will be her legacy for her children's future.

Stacey, whom Laurence calls "Hagar's spiritual grand-daughter" ("TYS" 22), counterpoints past and present in a series of memories indicated by indentation. Virtually every incident in Stacey's present triggers memories of her past self, as she attempts to come to terms with the mysteries of time and mutability.

FLASHFORWARDS: FUTURE SHOCK

Just as important as Stacey's memories of the past are her fantasies of the future — flashforwards, we could call them. Laurence counterpoints contemporary culture with visions of the future through Stacey's science-fiction fantasies. Stacey imagines herself on a distant planet called Zabyul, where she has sex with a galactic pilot named Jartek (93–94). She also has earth-threatening fantasies where Zuq plans the destruction of our planet (135–36). Stacey imagines that *"Very far away, in a galaxy countless light-years from this planet, a scorpion-tailed flower-faced film buff sits watching a nothing-shaped undulating screen. He decides he's seen enough. He switches off the pictures which humans always believed were themselves, and the imaginary planet known as Earth vanishes"* (77).

Stacey frequently envisions the future as a kind of dystopia, paralleling Luke Venturi's novel *The Greyfolk* (183–84) about life in America after a nuclear holocaust. Some of Stacey's fantasies depict a sinister future in a totalitarian city-state, prefiguring Margaret Atwood's dystopic novel *A Handmaid's Tale* (1985): *"The legions are marching tonight through the streets and their boot leather strikes hard against the pavements and there is nowhere to go but here"* (236). Stacey imagines:

> *The thin panthers are stalking the streets of the city, their claws unretracted after the cages of time and time again. The Roman legions are marching — listen to the hate-thudding of their boot leather. Strange things are happening, and the skeletal horsemen ride, ride, ride with all the winds of the world at their backs. There is nowhere to go this time* (85)

PRESENT TENSE: MASS MEDIA

Laurence makes skilful use of news via radio, television and newspapers to orient us in the quotidian actuality and in the historical view of contemporary culture, making this novel one of the most valuable records of the late sixties. "The Ever-Open Eye" (57) of television brings the political world right into Stacey's home and into the novel, reminding us of the war in Viet Nam, political violence in the far east, and racial violence in the U.S.A. The present appears so horrific that Stacey must escape the current via past memory or future fantasy.

Laurence also employs the titles of books, magazine articles, and adult education courses to colour in a broader cultural context. Stacey takes night courses in "Aspects of Contemporary Thought" (15) and "Varying Views of Urban Life" (69) and consumes magazine articles on contemporary families and newspaper articles about the degeneration of current culture. Stacey sings songs and hymns and recites prayers and nursery rhymes that help to relate the narrative to the broader cultural history that Laurence calls our "collective cultural memory" ("TNV" 156). Stacey's allusions to the Bible and

Greek mythology extend that referral scheme to a still more profound level of our communal consciousness.

DYNAMIC DEVELOPMENT:
CRESCENDO OF CATASTROPHES

The Fire-Dwellers demonstrates a distinctive rhythm — a dynamic
of conflict. Laurence's term is dilemma, and dilemma involves debate.
Consequently, all the characters, relationships and themes of the
novel are structured in conflict. Even the narrative method is structured around conflicts, as past wars with present and inner with
outer. Conflict causes crises, generating a dynamic narrative. Wis-
dom for Stacey consists of resolving those conflicts in the form of
reunions. So the rhythm of the narrative creates a movement from
denial to acceptance, from negation to affirmation, from pessimism
to guarded optimism.

The Fire-Dwellers is divided into ten chapters that structure the
narrative sequentially, delineating this development. Laurence introduces character and context — familial, temporal and geographical
— in the first chapter, as Stacey MacAindra faces a midlife identity
crisis in the heart of her family home on Bluejay Crescent in a modern
coastal city, "jewel of the Pacific Northwest" (10). Laurence creates
the conflicts economically in the second and third chapters, expand-
ing Stacey's ever-widening circle of acquaintance: Matthew Mac-
Aindra, Buckle Fennick, Tess Fogler, and even Thor Thorlakson are
all missing persons who have lost or mislaid their families and who
gravitate like magnets to the MacAindra hearth and home; even
Rachel and May Cameron are waiting in the wings in Manawaka,
only a letter away. The conflicts escalate in Chapter Four, as both
inner and outer reality impinge increasingly on Stacey's fragile psyche. As the chapters progress, pressure builds, exploding in a climax
which proves pivotal. Finally in Chapter Five, the precise middle of
the novel, a crisis constitutes the turning-point for the fire-dweller,
as Stacey resolves to seek salvation.

Chapters Six and Seven provide Stacey with a belated sentimental
education through her love affair with Luke Venturi, the catalytic
character. His counter-culture approach offers Stacey a perspective
on her situation that promotes her development. When he asks her
the existential question that men have asked women since Chaucer's

Loathly Lady — "What *do* you want?" (209) — she realizes that she does *not* want to run away from her responsibilities. Her decision, "I have to go home" (209), marks the turning-point in her resolution of her identity crisis.

Chapters Eight through Ten present a crescendo of catastrophes that confirm Stacey's choice: Buckle's death, Jen's trauma, Tess's attempted suicide, and Duncan's near-drowning break down the barriers, reunite the fragmented MacAindra family and show Stacey her real responsibilities as wife and mother. The tenth and final chapter depicts the denouement, as all difficulties are resolved, and Stacey overcomes her current crisis and finds the strength to face her future.

The novel ends like a soap opera, with protagonist and reader anticipating the next instalment with some trepidation: Stacey reflects, "Will the fires go on, inside and out? Until the moment when they go out for me, the end of the world. And then I'll never know what may happen in the next episode" (280). But will there be another episode? "She feels the city receding as she slides into sleep. Will it return tomorrow?" (281). Reassuring herself that *"Everything's all right,"* Stacey reflects, "Maybe the trivialities aren't so bad after all. They're something to focus on. As I'm forty tomorrow, that would be a good day to start a diet" (280). *The Fire-Dwellers* has come full circle, confirming the continuity of life, suggesting that we can anticipate *the same time tomorrow.*[7]

NETWORK OF IMAGERY: FIRE AND WATER

Laurence is an artistic writer who employs a network of imagery to symbolize her themes. In "Gadgetry or Growing" Laurence explains:

I am concerned mainly, I think, with finding a form which will enable a novel to reveal itself, a form through which the characters can breathe. When I try to think of form by itself, I have to put it in visual terms — I see it not like a house or a cathedral or any enclosing edifice, but rather as a forest, through which one can see outward, in which the shapes of trees do not prevent air

and sun, and in which the trees themselves are growing structures, something alive. That is, of course, an ideal, not something
that can ever be achieved. (81)

Laurence does achieve her artistic ideal, however, in *The Fire-
Dwellers*.

"WORLD ON FIRE"

Many great novels are constructed around a major symbol which acts
as the centre of a network of imagery that underlies the entire novel,
symbolizing its major themes — like a maypole surrounded by
circling and intertwining streamers. *The Fire-Dwellers* fits this pat-
tern perfectly. The dominant symbol of the novel is introduced in its
title. In "Living Dangerously . . . By Mail," Laurence tells how
furiously she defended her choice when her editor suggested changing her title:

> I instantly tapped out a five-page single-space communication
> on my typewriter transmitter, explaining why this was the only
> possible title. It had connotations of things like cave-dwellers
> and apartment-dwellers, the two most separate poles of our
> existence on earth. It also related to the verse from Sandburg's
> *Losers* which was quoted after the title page — "I who have
> fiddled in a world on fire." It related, as well, to Stacey's recur-
> ring thought about the nursery rhyme — "Ladybird, ladybird,
> fly away home / Your house is on fire, your children are gone."
> The fire theme threads through the novel, the fires being both
> inner and outer, and if we are to live in the present world, we
> must learn to live within the fires and still survive until we die.
> (*HS* 185)

As Laurence points out, the title image of the fire-dwellers is
echoed and emphasized by this epigraph to the novel drawn from
Carl Sandburg's poem *Losers*:

> *If I pass the burial spot of Nero*
> *I shall say to the wind, "Well, well"* —

I who have fiddled in a world on fire,
I who have done so many stunts not worth doing.

According to legend, Emperor Nero fiddled while Rome burned. In actuality, he "burned Christians like candles," as Laurence observes in "Sayonara, Agamemnon" (*HS* 19). Stacey says she has "this feeling like the fall of Rome" (117).

The fire symbol is applied explicitly to Stacey's situation as wife and mother on the very first page of *The Fire-Dwellers*:

Ladybird, ladybird,
Fly away home;
Your house is on fire,
Your children are gone. (7)

This insidious little rhyme, which serves to recall Stacey's maternal paranoia, is repeated at three significant points in the novel: at the beginning (7), the turning point (209) and the end (280), structuring the entire narrative. The significance of the rhyme is double-edged for Stacey, the original Ladybird, suggesting both her desire to escape from the trap of her four walls and her fear that providence will punish her for her sins through her children.

Stacey's world is on fire both literally and figuratively, internally and externally. Fiery by nature, Stacey was warned by her mother, *"Stacey, you have a terrible temper — you must learn to bank your fires"* (194), for "Irritation flares in her like a struck match" (64). But smothering her own flames proves difficult, surrounded as she is by flaming red-haired MacAindras indoors and "the eternal flames of the neon forest fires" (154) outdoors. Sexually stifled in her marriage, Stacey recalls, "Better to marry than burn, St. Paul said, but he didn't say what to do if you married *and* burned" (193). Stacey is burned literally when she scorches her hand on the red-hot burner of her stove when drunk.

But it is not just Stacey's inner world that is burning: the whole outer world is in flames, as the television constantly reminds us in capital letters:

EVER-OPEN EYE . . . MAN BURNING. HIS FACE CANNOT BE SEEN. HE LIES STILL, PERHAPS ALREADY DEAD. FLAMES LEAP AND QUIVER

FROM HIS BLACKENED ROBE LIKE EXCITED CHILDREN OF HELL.
VOICE: TODAY ANOTHER BUDDHIST MONK SET FIRE TO HIMSELF
IN PROTEST AGAINST THE WAR IN (116)

Closer to home, in the United States, cities are aflame with race riots:

EVER-OPEN EYE STREETS IN CITIES NOT SO FAR AWAY ARE BURN-
ING BURNING IN RAGE AND SORROW SET ABLAZE BY THE CHIL-
DREN OF SAMSON AGONISTES VOICE: RIOTS ARE SAID TO BE WELL
UNDER CONTROL IN (278)

"*Doom everywhere*" (58) is Stacey's impression, recalling "the fall of Rome" (117), when Nero fiddled. She watches transfixed as napalm spreads across an infant's face on a television newscast and listens appalled as a disembodied voice recounts another Vietnamese village torched or American city aflame.

As Stacey observes the city lights, "rearing neons in lightning strokes of color, jagged scarlet, blue like the crested heart of a flame" (43), she recalls the vision of the end of the world in the Redeemer's Advocate pamphlet, entitled "*God's War of the Last Day*" in "Ragged crimson letters like rising flames" (23). Stacey says, "I seem to believe in a day of judgement" (241) and wonders, "What will happen when the horsemen of the Apocalypse ride through this town?" (55). The theme of judgement is underlined by the motif of thunder and lightning, echoed in the name of Thor Thorlakson, the phoney "God of thunder" (244), and Valentine Tonnerre, French for thunder, who frees Stacey from her false god.

Stacey, the original sinner, fears that God's judgement will be visited on her through her vulnerable point, her children, hostages to fortune. Recalling the fire that burned Piquette Tonnerre with her children, Stacey fears the same fate for her own offspring: "Piquette and her kids, and the snow and fire. Ian and Duncan in a burning house" (241). A heavy smoker, Stacey fears she may cause the destruction of her house: "*The house is burning. Everything and everyone in it. Nothing can put out the flames. The house wasn't fire-resistant. One match was all it took*" (141) — recalling the Ladybird rhyme that haunts her. Stacey's first fantasy involves a forest fire: "*The hillside is burning. Who dropped a lighted cigarette? Did she? Evergreen catches fire with terrible ease*" (30).[18] Stacey can hear her children's voices calling to her from amid the flames, and she must traverse a tree bridge over a jagged rock canyon to reach them, but she can take only one *"away from the crackling smoke, back to the green world"* (31), while she hears the other three calling to her from the flames — Stacey's choice.

After Noah's Flood, God set a rainbow in the sky as a symbol of his promise never again to destroy the world with water. Instead, God will destroy the world with fire. Stacey's vision of the end of the world is of a fiery cataclysm — a fate that our current nuclear arms race renders all too possible. Explosions punctuate *The Fire-Dwellers*, as Stacey recalls her father Niall Cameron's story of the young boy caught between the legs by an exploding shell during World War I (10) and her husband Mac's story of the explosion that shattered an ancient Roman bridge and left him forever lumbered with Buckle Fennick (218).

Stacey's legacies from her dead father are, appropriately, firewater and firearms: after his funeral, she selects a flask and revolver from his effects. If the cataclysm occurs, Stacey can dispatch the merciful bullet to release her children, burned beyond recognition by radiation, from their sufferings (179).

Eventually, the purgatorial flames that persecute Stacey become a refining fire from which she will emerge, if not purified, at least tempered. She accepts that "to tell the truth the whole truth and nothing but the truth. . . . would set the house on fire" (257). After Mac confesses his own affair with Delores Appleton and affirms her innocence with Buckle, Stacey refrains from telling him about her own affair with Luke Venturi, but she feels like a Christian martyr: "Heap coals of fire on my head. I'm made of asbestos" (220).

Maybe Stacey is fireproof. Ultimately, she learns to live amid the flames of frenetic family life and the fires of contemporary culture. Falling asleep at the end of the narrative, she reflects, "Will the fires go on, inside and out? Until the moment when they go out for me, the end of the world" (280).

WATERS OF REDEMPTION

The antidote to fire is water, the only element that can vanquish flame.[19] After trying to drown her sorrows in spirits, Stacey awakens with a hangover, thinking, "Help. Water. Water. I'm dying of thirst" (104). Her need for healing water is spiritual as well as physical, however. If Stacey's nightmares feature fire, her daydreams involve water. Whenever the flames get too hot, Stacey heads for the seashore for solace for her scorched soul. Stacey lives in the "jewel of the Pacific Northwest" (10), and whenever she escapes from her "Home Sweet Home" (104), she runs for the waterfront, where she admires the freeflying gulls and watches the "black rusty freighters doing their imitations of monolithic ghosts, clanking and groaning" (13) in the harbour, as "the vessels move in ponderously to be unladen like great sea cows swimming in to be milked" (237).

Water is Stacey's natural element: always a strong swimmer, she feels like a mermaid out of her element in the flames of frenetic family life and chaotic contemporary culture. Her lover Luke calls her "merwoman" (178) — appropriately, for Stacey's thoughts are free-floating, like seaweed under water:

Everything drifts. Everything is slowly swirling, philosophies tangled with the grocery lists, unreal-real anxieties like rose thorns waiting to tear the uncertain flesh, nonentities of thoughts floating like plankton, green and orange particles, seaweed — lots of that, dark purple and waving, sharks with fins like cutlasses, herself held underwater by her hair, snared around auburn-rusted anchor chains (34)

Stacey's happiest memories are of lakes, punctuating the precious moments of her life. Driven to distraction by four children, she remembers her youthful self swimming alone and free at Diamond Lake (161). Desperate to get through to Mac, she recalls her first idyllic love-making with the airman from Montreal on the shores of Diamond Lake, "with the lapping of the lake in their heads" (72), while "The path of the moon lighted the black lake. The fishes danced and the night birds dipped and pirouetted in obeisance towards the fallen light, the shreds of heaven" (71). Rejected by her husband, she relives their Edenic honeymoon at Timber Lake, with "Spruce trees darkly still in the sun, and the water so clear you could see the grey-gold minnows flickering," where she said to Mac, "I like everything about you," and he replied, *"That's good, honey. I like everything about you, too"* (176). Rejected by her daughter, Stacey recalls the lake where Katie was conceived, "The pine and spruce harps in the black ground outside, in the dark wind from the lake that never penetrated the narrow-windowed cabin. Their skins slippery with sweat together, slithering as though with some fine and pleasurable oil. Stacey knowing his moment and her own as both separate and unseparable" (128). Rejected by her two young sons, Stacey remembers "Duncan and Ian last summer at the beach, wrestling and wisecracking, brown skinny legs and arms, the shaggy flames of their hair, their skin smelling of sand and salt-water. Sea-children, as though they should have been crowned with fronds of kelp and ridden dolphins" (73) — offspring of the merwoman. When she imagines escaping to some promised fantasy land, it is to a dream lake in the cool Cariboo (161).

Stacey's dream lakes are the setting for a cluster of images of seabirds and goldfish. Birds symbolize the spirit of freedom for Stacey. The original Ladybird (a bird of a very different feather), Stacey escapes from the urban flames of Bluejay Crescent to watch the free gulls flying on the waterfront:

> The gulls are spinning high, freewheeling. Wings like white arcs of light crescenting above the waterfront. Voices mocking piratically at the city's edges. . . . If they're prophets in bird form, they might as well save their breath. They aren't prophets, though. They only look it, angelic presences and voices like gravel out of a grave. Birds in prophet form. (12–13)

Birds are voices from another world, as Stacey recalls "the lunatic voices of the loons, witch birds out there in the night lake, or voices of dead shamans, mourning the departed Indian gods" (159). The hymn "God sees the little sparrow fall" (67) and the picture of "a sweetly innocuous and vacant-faced St. Francis surrounded by feathered companions" (68) suggest that "God's in his heaven all's right with the world" (63). But birds can symbolize death, as they do in *A Bird in the House*, where "A bird in the house means a death in the house" (102). Stacey fears "the tomb birds, scaring the guts out of me with their vulture wings" (270). Goldfish, seemingly symbolic of domestic innocence, also turn out to be emblematic of destruction, as Tess Fogler's pet fish, barracuda in disguise, kill and devour one another, prompting Stacey's vision of a Darwinian struggle for the survival of the fittest: "Dog eat dog and fish eat fish" (92).

Stacey's lover Luke, a fisherman named for the Apostle, his house filled with fishnets, seems to Stacey "like the rain in a dry year" (187). Luke calls Stacey "merwoman" (166) and invites her to sail out to sea in "the cockleshell that we jokingly refer to as a boat" (206). Surnamed Venturi, suggesting adventure, Luke offers to fulfil her escape fantasy by taking her north to Cariboo country. A fisher of souls, he invites Stacey to blissful oblivion by crossing the Skeena River on a ferry driven by a Charon figure — the boatman who ferried dead souls across the River Styx to the underworld in Greek myth. Stacey longs to go *where the rivers speed and thunder while the ancient-eyed boatman waits*" (222), but she fears the freedom symbolized by the free-flowing river.

Stacey recognizes that escape will not bring salvation. The life-giving waters of redemption must be discovered within, if she is to be able to survive the flames of life. In the depths of her despair, overwhelmed by grief, Stacey is blinded by tears of sympathy for Matthew, when he repeats the Psalm, "*Save me, O God, for the waters are come in unto my soul*" (152). But Stacey does not drown; instead, she suffers a significant sea change — a "change of heart" (221).

But water can be hostile to life, and the sea can kill, as Stacey realizes: "I wonder how deep it is, at the deepest? How far out does it go? How many creatures does it contain, not just the little shells and the purple starfish and the kelp, but all the things that live a long way out? Deathly embracing octopus in the south waters, the white whales spouting in the only-half-melted waters of the north, the sharks knowing nothing except how to kill" (271–72). The motif of drowning is not yet finished, for her favourite, Duncan, is almost drowned at the seashore. Blinded by salt tears, Stacey watches the seawater pump from his mouth until she hears him utter the infant wail of a newborn (267–68).[20]

In a moment of truth inspired by Duncan's brush with death, Mac confronts his ultimate fear, Stacey's suicide stunt, and asks her what she did with her father's old war revolver. Rejecting "*Pre-Mourning*" (253) in favour of affirmation, Stacey threw the gun into Timber Lake, drowning death, like Ethel Wilson's "Swamp Angel" — a modern Excalibur (279). Vancouver is hardly Avalon, but Stacey realizes that she can live there without going under or going up in flames.

Since the flames of *The Fire-Dwellers* suggest the fires of hell and the lakes suggest the waters of redemption, we may expect to encounter Christian symbolism in this novel. Laurence confesses that "I do not really believe that God is totally dead in our universe" and "I am a Christian in the sense of my heritage" (DCI 111–12). Stacey no longer believes in "the Stations of the Cross" (68), but she confides in God nevertheless, even though she maintains, like her sister Rachel in *A Jest of God*, that "God has a sick sense of humour" (72).

Judging by the theory that what we swear by reveals what we truly respect, Stacey does respect God, however, for she takes His name in vain regularly, swearing "In God's name" (117) and calling on "Jesus lover of my soul" (35). Imagining her own death, she wishes she could utter the Christian prayer, "Holy Mary, Mother of God, be with me now and in the hour of my death" (120).

Stacey, the original sinner, has a strong sense of guilt and fears that God may punish her for her sins through her most vulnerable point, her children, hostages to fortune. She demonstrates a Calvinistic sense of original sin: *"Mea culpa"* (106) is her motto. When Duncan almost drowns in the sea, Stacey prays, "God, let him be all right, and I'll never want to get away again, I promise. If it was anything I did, take it out on me, not on him — that's too much punishment for me" (267). Stacey fears the Judgement of God (14): "I seem to believe in a day of judgement" (241), she acknowledges. She wonders "What will happen when the horsemen of the Apocalypse ride through this town?" (55). She views Thor as the "god of thunder" (45), the pagan god of vengeance. When Mac gets a new job, Stacey feels "As though I'd been forgiven after all" (34).

Stacey acknowledges that she is very superstitious. When Duncan almost drowns, she screams, *"Duncan! You've got to be all right,"* but she is "aware of the words' total lie. They are rune words, trinket charms to ward off the evil eye" (267). After Duncan is saved, she acknowledges her superstitions:

— Judgement. All the things I don't like to think I believe in. But at the severe moments, up they rise, the tomb birds, scaring the guts out of me with their vulture wings. Maybe it's as well to know they're there. Maybe knowing might help to keep them at least a little in their place. Or maybe not. I used to think about Buckle that he was as superstitious as a caveman. I didn't know then that I was too. (270)

Stacey has a Manichaean view of the universe — that is, a moral scheme with gods and devils, or principles of good and evil. She swears by "Ye gods" (273) and takes a course in "Man and His Gods" (52). She also believes in angels and demons. She calls her daughter "angel bud" (265) and sings a hymn that invokes "*Ye holy angels bright / Who wait at God's right hand*" (68).

Stacey wishes that "all demons would be laid to rest" (193), and views Thor as an arch-demon, a "refugee from the discards of Lucifer's army" (100). But when she penetrates his thunder-god disguise, she is disappointed: "If we're scared, at least there is some dignity in being scared of genuine demons. Aren't there any demons left in hell? How in hell can we live without them?" (245).

Stacey also sees herself as a kind of Christ figure, bearing the stigmata of the Crucifixion. She jokes with Thor about his quiz: "I find I got stigmata on both palms and I gotta wear gloves everywhere I go, you think I'm gonna *say*?" (101). Later he jokes, "No more stigmata ha-ha?" (229). Well might Stacey reply, "Ha bloody ha" (100), because she has been branded by her stove: "Two red crescent lines have appeared on the skin of her left palm" — "My brand of stigmata. My western brand. The Double Crescent" (130). Maybe Stacey is the "Crucified Woman" (*DE* 15). Perhaps she represents the Second Coming which she challenged God to send down: next time "get It born as a her with seven young" (156).

REFLECTIONS ON MIRROR IMAGES:
"MIRROR, MIRROR, ON THE WALL"

Mirror imagery is central to Laurence's theme of identity. The novel opens with Stacey reflecting on her image in the mirror: "The full-length mirror is on the bedroom door. Stacey sees images reflected there, distanced by the glass like humans on TV, less real than real and yet more sharply focused because isolated and limited by a frame" (7). Photographs parallel mirrors because both reflect pictures of the self, except mirrors reflect the present and pictures the past, emphasizing the concepts of time and mutability. Stacey compares the reflection of her present middle-aged self in the mirror with the representation of her past youthful self in her wedding photograph: "Stacey sees mirrored her own self in the present flesh" (8), compared to the photograph showing "Stacey twenty-three, almost beautiful although not knowing it then" (8). Stacey "strips and looks at herself in the full-length mirror" (20) and recalls her photograph album: "when I saw a snapshot of myself, years ago, I thought *My heavens, I was actually pretty — why didn't I know it then?*" (21).

Stacey "sits on the bed and looks at herself in the full-length mirror" (203) to hold dialogues with her self, symbolizing her sense of her schizoid psyche. She also looks in the mirror "to make sure I'm really there" (132). Luke says, "if I look very hard, I can just about make you out in there, but miniature, like looking through the wrong end of a telescope" (167).

Laurence also compares mirrors to television on the opening page of the novel, for "The Ever-Open Eye" (57) shows us pictures of people who might be us. Stacey identifies with the newspaper photograph of a mother holding her dead child: "The woman's mouth open wide — a sound of unbearability but rendered in silence by the camera clicking. Only the zero mouth to be seen, noiselessly proclaiming the gone-early child" (254). Stacey also identifies with newspaper photographs and television pictures of mothers whose children are killed, as Laurence's "Open Letter to the Mother of Joe Bass" vividly verifies (*HS* 200).

Television mirrors reality, Stacey realizes, as she compares the fictional violence of Western serials with the actual violence of Viet Nam newscasts: "The program ends, and then the News. This time the bodies that fall stay fallen. *Flicker-flicker-flicker.* From one dimension to another. Stacey does not know whether Ian and Duncan, when they look, know the difference" (57).

Other characters act as metaphorical mirrors for Stacey. After she dances secretly to her old "*Tommy Dorsey Boogie*" (124) and espies Katie dancing to her own music in her own idiom, she realizes that she is an outmoded model (125–27). All of Stacey's friends, from Tess Fogler to Bertha Garvey, reflect facets of Stacey's situation. Her encounter with Valentine Tonnerre, a ghost from her Manawaka past, makes Stacey recognize her own good fortune (241).

Just as the mountains surrounding Vancouver, still snow-covered in summer, suggest to Stacey that this "jewel of the Pacific Northwest" (10) partakes of "two worlds, two simultaneous seasons" (69), so Stacey lives in two worlds with two simultaneous seasons — the real winter world and the world of the imagination, where it is always summer. Laurence symbolizes the inner and outer worlds of imagination and actuality through imagery of nature and artifice. Stacey, like Laurence, loves the countryside and loathes the urban jungle. Trapped in the suburbs, Stacey dreams of escaping to silent snowy mountains (14) or northern lakes surrounded by evergreens (161). Vegetation frames the pictures of her imagination, as she envisions "Jungles of blackberry bushes and salmonberry. Spruce trees darkly still in the sun, and the water so clear you could see the grey-gold minnows flickering" (176) and hears "The pine and spruce harps in the black ground outside, in the dark wind from the lake" (128).

Flowers are symbolic for Stacey also, suggested by the fact that she calls her youngest child Jennifer her "flower" (93). Flowers frame some of Stacey's precious memories, as she recalls Mac bringing her two dozen yellow chrysanthemums when Jen was born (24). When she visits Luke for the last time, Stacey wears a dress the colour of bronze, "like those chrysanthemums in fall" (206). Thor's Richalife party sports "potted rhododendrons [that] still bear the brown corpses of this spring's flowering" (228), revealing the moribund nature of the enterprise.

Many characters construct masks to hide behind or create caves to hide in. People's double monikers signify their dual personalities: Stacey is Anastasia (90), Mac is Clifford (64), Buckle is Arbuckle (54), and Thor Thorlakson is really Vernon Winkler (243). Everybody has something to hide, it appears.

Characters create masks from makeup, recalling the actors' masks in Greek drama or bear masks of Indian totems (162). Valentine Tonnerre paints a lipsticked cupid's bow over her real mouth, like a comic mask superimposed over a tragic one (239). Tess Fogler hopes to hide her neuroses behind her Queen Hatshepsut cosmetics. Her façade is effective: Stacey thinks, "I look at her, done up like a Christmas present, and I wonder what's actually inside. Maybe nothing" (169–70). Stacey recalls her own face distorted by drunkenness into "a swollen mask like the face of a woman drowned, the features blurred" (107). Recalling her father's death mask, Stacey reflects, "Perhaps it isn't that the masks have been put on, one for each year like the circles that tell the age of a tree. Perhaps they've been gradually peeled off, and what's there underneath is the face that's always been there for me, the unspeaking eyes, the mouth for whom words were too difficult" (157). As the layers peel off, vulnerability is revealed beneath the veneer.

Characters employ clothing as camouflage. Stacey wears her hat and veil "as a disguise" (132) to hide her identity: "*Under this chapeau lurks a mermaid, a whore, a tigress*" (15), she crows. She imagines she wears gloves to conceal her stigmata, signs of her paranoia, and wishes for a zippered kaftan to hide her stretch marks, emblems of maternity, when she makes love with Luke (187).

Characters also hide in caves: Stacey reflects, "I sometimes see us like moles, living in our underground burrows, with eyes that can't stand any light" (151). Mac is a cave-dweller who has gone "underground, living in his own caves" (24), and "finds his exit" (30) in the cell of his self where no one can follow. But Stacey is also a cave-dweller who wants to bury herself in a snowy mountain cave (14). Luke exhorts, "Come out. From wherever you're hiding yourself" (167). Stacey thinks, "*If only I could get out.* What if everybody is thinking that, in some deep half-buried cave of themselves?" (231).

Initially, Stacey considers her house on Bluejay Crescent a "fortress, which I'd like to believe strong" (18), holding the world out. But eventually she believes her "boundaries are four walls" (69), where "I'm trapped" (194). Finally, she realizes, "I was wrong to think of the trap as the four walls. It's the world" (276). But Stacey is wrong: the trap is the cell of the self.

Caves can become prisons when the characters are caught in traps of their own creating. Stacey reflects, "It's like being inside a balloon made out of some kind of glue, and when you try to get out, you only get tangled and stuck" (123). She feels she is observing the world "through some thick and isolating glass barrier or like TV with the voices turned off" (93) — like Sylvia Plath's *Bell Jar*. Stacey imagines that the hairdryer at the beauty salon is a chrysalis, a cocoon from which she will emerge as a beautiful butterfly (93).

Characters conceal their real feelings in metaphorical suitcases, "mental baggage" (192) or "invisible garbage" (113), impeding their progress: "Too much mental baggage," Stacey realizes; "Things keep spilling out of the suitcases, taking me by surprise, bewildering me as I stand on the platform" (38). Finally Stacey realizes that Mac has his own burdens: "we carry our own suitcases. How was it I never knew how many you were carrying? Too busy toting my own" (220).

THE ARTISTRY OF ALLUSION: "MEMORY-HERITAGE"

Margaret Laurence incorporates, even in her most contemporary writing, the "memory-heritage" of our culture, the past "which has become legend, the past of a collective cultural memory" ("TNV" 156). The Bible is a major repository of that communal memory, and Laurence is steeped in biblical lore. She declares:

> There's a great deal, for example, in the Bible which really hits me very hard; it seems to express certain symbolic truths about the human dilemma and about mankind. The expression of various facets of human life and of human life searching for a consciousness greater than its own — that is, in God — some of this moves me in the way that great poetry moves you. I'm particularly attached to the King James version of the Bible, because it *is* the poetry of it that really hits me. A great many of the characters feel as I do about it: there's an enormous emotional inheritance. I am a Christian in the sense of my heritage. (DCI 112)

BIBLICAL ALLUSIONS: PEOPLE AND PARABLES

Related to the religious imagery discussed earlier are allusions to people and parables from the Bible. Stacey compares herself and Mac to Adam and Eve, creation's first husband-and-wife team (155), recalling Milton's *Paradise Lost*. Stacey also compares their sons, Ian and Duncan, to Adam and Eve's sons, Cain and Abel: when Ian and Duncan squabble, Stacey reflects, "Cain and his brother must have started their hatred like this" (19). According to the Old Testament, Cain, Adam and Eve's eldest son, became jealous of his younger brother Abel because Abel's burnt offerings were accepted by God in preference to his own; so Cain killed Abel and became the world's first murderer (Genesis 4: 1–15).

Implicit is the parallel of Stacey and her sister Rachel to Rachel and Leah in Genesis, a parallel that is made explicit in Rachel's story, *A Jest of God*: "when the LORD saw that Leah *was* hated, he opened her womb, but Rachel *was* barren" (29: 31). "AND when Rachel saw that she bare Jacob no children, Rachel envied her sister; and said unto Jacob, Give me children, or else I die" (30: 1). Like Rachel and Leah, Stacey is fertile, while Rachel is barren — and jealous.

Mac's father Matthew, named for the Apostle, is compared by Stacey to Moses, who was given the Ten Commandments by Jehovah on Mount Sinai, but died before he could lead his people, the enslaved Jews, out of Egypt and across the River Jordan into the Promised Land, as chronicled in Exodus. Stacey imagines *"Matthew, towering like Moses, bearing in his eyes the letter of the Law"* (121). Stacey remembers her youthful self having "breasts like apples as it says in the Song of Solomon" (11). When she contemplates the degeneration of her marriage, however, she thinks she should "wail like the widows of Ashur" (38). The moment when Matthew quotes the Psalm, *"Save me, O God, for the waters are come in unto my soul"* (152) proves a turning-point for Stacey, prompting spiritual salvation.

Stacey thinks of the noise at the Richalife party as a "babel of voices" (231), alluding to the Tower of Babel parable in Genesis 11:1–9. The people aspired to build a tower that would reach to heaven; God prevented their plan and punished their hubris by confounding their speech so that they could not understand one another: "Therefore is the name of it called Babel; because the LORD did there confound the language of all the earth: and from thence did the LORD scatter them abroad upon the face of all the earth" (11:9). The Tower of Babel symbolizes the theme of failure of communication in *The Fire-Dwellers*.

The Ever-Open Eye of Stacey's television records cities "SET ABLAZE BY THE CHILDREN OF SAMSON AGONISTES" (278). The Book of Judges chronicles the life of Samson and his imprisonment by the Philistines at Gaza and betrayal by his wife Delilah. John Milton wrote a dramatic poem called *Samson Agonistes* or Samson the Wrestler, published in 1671 with *Paradise Regained*, modeled on Greek tragedy.

Emperor Nero, alluded to in the epigraph to the novel drawn from Carl Sandburg's poem "Losers," fiddled while Rome burned, according to legend. Emperor of the Roman Empire from 37 to

68 A.D., Nero was renowned for his cruelty. He "burned Christians like candles" (*HS* 28), as Laurence points out in her essay "Sayonara, Agamemnon." His cruelty precipitated a palace mutiny at home in Rome and revolts against the Roman Empire abroad. Rome is referred to repeatedly throughout *The Fire-Dwellers*, for Stacey considers that contemporary culture seems "like the fall of Rome" (117). She imagines the invasion of the Goths (179) and dreams of Roman legions: "*The legions are marching tonight through the streets and their boot leather strikes hard against the pavements and there is nowhere to go but here*" (236). She wonders "What will happen when the horsemen of the Apocalypse ride through this town?" (55), echoing the book of Revelations.

The Christian religion arose out of this Roman Empire. Christ is referred to frequently throughout *The Fire-Dwellers*. Stacey and Mac take Christ's name in vain, swearing "by Christ" and "for Christ's sake" (75). Luke Venturi imagines his father, a provider of wine, as "*Christ in Concrete*," squashed by his own grape-crusher — although "he couldn't visualize himself in a star role. One of the lesser apostles, you might say" (183). Luke is named for Christ's disciple, author of a Gospel of the New Testament recording the life of Christ.

Stacey views herself as a Christ figure branded by the stigmata of Christ's crucifixion, imagining that "I got stigmata on both palms" (101). When she burns her hand on the stove, "Two red crescent lines have appeared on the skin of her left palm," which Stacey interprets as "My brand of stigmata. My western brand. The Double Crescent" (130) — making her a "Crucified Woman" (*DE* 15).

GREEK MYTHOLOGY: FIGURES AND FANTASIES

Closely related to the biblical allusions are Laurence's allusions to Greek mythology. Again, Laurence employs family dynasties to parallel the MacAindras. Stacey used to view Mac as "Agamemnon King of Men" (181), hero of Greek tragedy. But now Stacey sympathizes with Agamemnon's wife, Clytemnestra, who murdered her husband, because he "sacrificed their youngest daughter for success in war" (33).

Aeschylus' dramatic trilogy, *The Oresteia*, begins with Agamemnon setting sail for the Trojan War to rescue Helen, wife of his brother Menelaus, who has eloped with Paris, son of King Priam of Troy. To propitiate the gods and bring favourable winds, Agamemnon sacrifices his daughter Iphigenia. In vengeance, Clytemnestra, with her lover Aegisthus, murders her husband when he returns from Troy with the captured daughter of King Priam, the prophetess Cassandra. Clytemnestra is murdered in turn by her son Orestes in revenge for his father.

"Sayonara, Agamemnon" records Laurence's feelings at the Lion Gate where Agamemnon's chariot passed on the way home to Mycenae from Troy, as "Agamemnon, King of Men, mounted the winding path that led him to his palace and his death":

> It was easy to imagine the king, a warrior by skill and a warrior in his concepts, expecting a pleased pride from his queen. And her, terrified, but with the memory of the child burning at her, their youngest child whom the king had sacrificed to the gods for luck in war. Even as she greeted him, this memory had been compelling her towards the revenge that would have no ending, but would finally be turned against her as she died at the hands of her son. (*HS* 22)

The fact that the book lying on Stacey's night table is Frazer's *The Golden Bough* (8) indicates that mythology, the subject of Frazer's influential study, published in twelve volumes between 1890 and 1915, will be a significant factor in *The Fire-Dwellers*. Stacey compares herself to mythical figures like Medusa: when she feels her worries "churning around like a covey of serpents" in her guts, she thinks, "— Medusa does in summer wear a nest of serpents in her hair" (106). Medusa, one of three sister Gorgons, monsters of the underworld, had hair formed of serpents and a face so ugly that all who saw it were turned to stone. Even more significant is Luke's comparison of the ancient boatman who drives people across the Skeena River to Charon, who ferried dead souls across the Rivers Styx and Acheron to the underworld in ancient Greek mythology (208).

Queen Hatshepsut, an Egyptian Pharaoh, plays a part, for the cosmetics that Tess Fogler shows Stacey are named after her. Tess explains, "Queen Hatshepsut. She was very famous. She ruled as pharaoh in her own right" (172). Jake Fogler insists, "she was famous for her cruelty and she dressed as a man and married her stepson or some such relative and he hated her so much he had her name chiseled off all the monuments after she died" (172). Encyclopedias tell another story:

> Queen of Egypt (c. 1490–1468 BC) of the 18th dynasty. The half-sister and widow of Thutmose II, she overshadowed the young Thutmose III, and assumed the status of pharaoh. During her reign direct communications with Punt (now S Eritrea) were reopened. Illustrated accounts of her expedition there and of the transport of her obelisks from Aswan are carved on her funerary temple at Dayr al-Bahri. After her death Thutmose III attempted to obliterate her memory by defacing her monuments.[21]

Laurence refers to Hatshepsut in "Captain Pilot Shawkat and Kipling's Ghost," an essay about her trip through the Aswan dam: "The redoubtable Queen Hatshepsut, who ruled as pharaoh in her own right, sent her ships by way of this canal, about 1495 B.C., on one of the world's first trade missions, to the east coast of Africa" (HS 115). Hatshepsut is clearly a feminist model, like Boadicea.

LITERARY ALLUSIONS: "THIS IS THE WAY THE WORLD ENDS"

There are fewer literary allusions in *The Fire-Dwellers* than in Laurence's other novels, perhaps because Stacey is only "Self-educated, but zanily" (33). She says "Neither Mac nor I could have mustered more than about two lines of Shakespeare" (59). Luke paraphrases T.S. Eliot's 1925 poem "The Hollow Men" when he asks if Stacey planned to dispatch herself with her father's revolver "when the Goths' chariots and the final bill came in, or when some evangelist corporal decided this is the way the world ends not with a whimper but a bang?" (179).

Perhaps it is no coincidence that the television show that Mac and Stacey watch features Robin Hood, legendary folk-hero of fifteenth-century ballads, such as the *Lytell Geste of Robyn Hoode* (c. 1495), who stole from the rich to give to the poor. The movie makes the son of Robin Hood the instigator of Magna Carta, the document signed by King John of England in 1215, confirming political rights: "EVER-OPEN EYE THE SON OF ROBIN HOOD STANDS BEHIND KING JOHN AT RUNNYMEDE, MAKING THE RELUCTANT MONARCH SIGN THE MAGNA CARTA" (120). If Robin Hood was a folk-hero of the 1400s, could his son have been involved with the Magna Carta in 1215? Magna Carta remains the source of civil rights, a contested issue in the nineteen-sixties.

The night courses Stacey takes emphasize significant aspects of the novel: "Man and His Gods" (52) underlines the religious theme, "Ancient Greek Drama" (33) reinforces the mythological element, and "Aspects of Contemporary Thought" (15) emphasizes the importance of modern culture for the fire-dwellers.

SONGS, HYMNS, AND NURSERY RHYMES: "ASSIST OUR SONG"

Laurence employs songs, hymns, and nursery rhymes significantly in *The Fire-Dwellers*. Most significant is the nursery rhyme that opens the novel:

Ladybird, ladybird,
Fly away home;
Your house is on fire,
Your children are gone. (7)

Laurence repeats this lethal little ditty at the beginning, turning point (209), and conclusion (280) of the novel, punctuating the development of the narrative. Stacey recalls another nursery rhyme, "Here is a candle to light you to bed, and here comes a chopper to chop off your head," reflecting, "Just the thing to make the sprouts sleep soundly, especially if followed by that prayer about if I should die before I wake." She judges, "Maybe it's okay, though. Prepares them for what they can expect" (7). Thus Laurence prepares the reader for a picture of gloom and doom. Later, when Stacey imagines death, she recalls the prayer, "Holy Mary, Mother of God, be with me now and in the hour of my death" (120).

Stacey's salvation is inspired by hymns: after Duncan says they sang "God sees the little sparrow fall" (67) at Sunday school, Stacey sings another hymn:

Ye holy angels bright
Who wait at God's right hand
Or through the realms of light
Fly at your Lord's command,
Assist our song,
Or else the theme too high doth seem
For mortal tongue. (68)

Margaret Laurence comments on the power of hymns: "Part of the terrific impact of things like the hymns derives from the fact that you learned these things in a much earlier era of your life, an era of rock-solid faith. Now you *lost* this: and part of the impact is not that you believe it, but you mourn your disbelief. This is Eden lost" (DCI 112). Perhaps that is why singing this hymn inspires Stacey's first tears, sign of the redemptive flood of her eventual salvation.

Later Stacey sings a saccharine song reminiscent of a hymn:

There's a gold mine in the sky
Faraway —
We will go there, you and I,
Some sweet day,
And we'll say hello to friends who said goodbye,
When we find that long lost gold mine in the sky.
Faraway, faraw-a-ay — (129)

But Stacey denies this phoney vision of heavenly bliss, because she believes that "there's no gold mine in the sky" (129). Later, she paraphrases the hymn, "Dear Lord and Father of mankind, forgive our foolish ways, as some goon once said. Reclothe us in our rightful mind" (263) — perhaps as a half-hearted prayer.

Laurence includes war songs, since war is a major subject of her concern. Stacey recalls the Queen's Own Cameron Highlanders marching through Manawaka, during World War II, preceded by Highland pipers playing *The March of the Cameron Men*. After Dieppe, where many of the boys she knew were killed, the march became a pibroch for them and induced mourning in her forever after (217). Stacey is "Conned into memory" (72) of her love affair with the airman from Montreal stationed in Manawaka during the war when the Supermarket Musak plays:

I'll be seeing you
In all the old familiar places — (71)

During the Peace March Stacey attends, the marchers sing two sixties war-protest songs, "We Shall Overcome" and "Where Have All the Flowers Gone" (251–52).

Richalife apes religion in its ritualistic rallies and hymn-like songs:

Richness is a quality of living,
Richness quells the trouble and the strife,
Richness is the being and the giving,
Anyone can reach a Richalife. (133)

Laurence satirizes the phoniness of such imitation religions. Similarly, Stacey sees beauty salons as modern temples, where "The priestesses are clad in pale mauve smocks" like clerical vestments to offer "the benediction of the shampoo" (93). Stacey sees supermarkets as temples in the new religion of commercialism: "The long aisles of the temple. Side chapels with the silver-flash of chrome where the dead fish lie among the icy strawberries. The mounds of offerings, yellow planets of grapefruit, jungles of lettuce, tentacles of green onions, Arctic effluvia flavored raspberry. . . . Music hymning from invisible choirs" (71).

Music is very important to the MacAindras, as it is to Margaret Laurence. Stacey likes to dance, as Laurence did herself, according to her memoirs (*DE* 18). Stacey dances to "*Tommy Dorsey Boogie,*" remnant of her Manawaka teens, when she used to dance in the Flamingo Dance Hall: "Dance hope, girl, dance hurt" (125). When Stacey spies Katie dancing alone to her own idiom, she realizes that her dancing days are over: "from now on, the dancing goes on only in the head. . . . Well, in the head isn't such a terrible place to dance" (276). Stacey imagines dancing to "Zorba's Dance," a celebration of life: "*She is dancing alone.*"

She starts slowly, following the beat of the music, her bare feet
certain, confident. The sudden upswirling of the tune, and she is
whirling, wrists gyrating, possessed by the god. Swifter, swifter,
with the freedom of wild horses, the music races the wind. Then
he is beside her, the man who also is enabled to hear the music,
who also is directed by the god (275–76)

Laurence entitled her memoirs *Dance on the Earth*. She writes, "I have countless foremothers. I never saw my mothers dancing. But now I know their dance" (19). Laurence has made her dance of life part of our "memory-heritage" ("TNV" 156).

Because Stacey is in such close touch with popular culture through her children and her own childhood, Laurence can capture both the contemporary context and our cultural heritage in *The Fire-Dwellers* through her artistry of allusion.

[1] Joan Coldwell, "Laurence, Margaret," *The Oxford Companion to Canadian Literature*, 434.

[2] "The Road Not Taken" is the title of a poem by Robert Frost.

[3] "Only connect . . ." is the epigraph to E.M. Forster's 1910 novel *Howard's End*.

[4] Nora Foster Stovel, in "Sisters, Structures and Symbols: *A Jest of God* and *The Fire-Dwellers*," forthcoming in *Margaret Laurence: Fiction and Fact*, edited by Greta Coger, compares Laurence's sister novels in these respects.

[5] "Lady Lazarus" is the title of a poem by Sylvia Plath.

[6] This phrase is from the poem "Fern Hill" by Dylan Thomas.

[7] The concluding refrain of "The Ladies" by Rudyard Kipling reads: "*For the Colonel's Lady an' Judy O'Grady / Are sisters under their skins!*"

[8] Stacey's statement to Mac echoes Nick Kazlik's warning to Rachel: "I'm not God. I can't solve anything" (*JG* 148). Laurence insists that, as a novelist, you "realize that you are *not* God" (DCI 104).

[9] The hero of Laurence's children's book *Jason's Quest* is a picaro named Jason, a mole who quests for a cure to the ailment that plagues Molanium.

[10] Margaret Drabble said that her novel *The Middle Ground* (1980) was about "the middle years, caught between children and parents, free of neither."

[11] At the end of Ethel Wilson's novel *Swamp Angel* (1954), Maggie Vardoe hurls the "Swamp Angel," which is a small revolver, into Three Loon Lake (157).

[12] "Let It Be" is the title of a Beatles song that appeared in 1970.

[13] "Words alone are certain good" is a line from William Butler Yeats's poem "The Song of the Happy Shepherd" from *Crossways* (1889).

[14] Sylvia Plath's autobiographical novel *The Bell Jar* (1963) employs the central image of the bell jar as a symbol of the suicidal heroine's isolation.

[15] In George Orwell's 1949 dystopic novel *Nineteen Eighty-four*, posters featuring an enormous face sport the caption, "BIG BROTHER IS WATCHING YOU" (Harmondsworth, Eng.: Penguin, 1954), 5.

[16] Virginia Woolf, *To the Lighthouse* (New York: Harcourt, 1927), 306.

[17] Several contemporary women's novels demonstrate this circular structure, including Doris Lessing's *The Summer Before the Dark* (1973) and Margaret Drabble's *The Middle Ground* (1980), where the narrative ends much as it began, with little external change, but immense internal development for the heroine. Drabble's novel also features the soap-opera ending noted in *The Fire-Dwellers*: "A child calls her from downstairs. The door bell rings. The telephone also rings. She hears her house living. She rises" (248) — suggesting continuation.

[18] Laurence recounts an anecdote about a meeting where she inadvertently set fire to a tablecloth by smoking surreptitiously under its cover (*DE* 215).

[19] George Woodcock argues, in "The Human Elements: Margaret Laurence's Fiction" in *The World of Canadian Writing* (1980), that each of Laurence's

Manawaka novels is structured around one of the four elements, fire being the central element in *The Fire-Dwellers*..

[20] Laurence's poem "For my Daughter on her Twenty-sixth Birthday" says, "And my man your father / drew us to shore and breath / a quarter century ago" (*DE* 251), suggesting that this episode in the novel is drawn from life.

[21] *The New Universal Family Encyclopedia* (N.Y.: Random, 1985), 446–47.

Works Cited

Anonymous. "The Fire-dwellers." *Booklist* 65 (15 June 1969): 1165.
Brief positive review.
_____ . "Other New Novels." *Times Literary Supplement* 22 May 1969: 563.
Rpt. in New, 197.
Dismissive review of *The Fire-Dwellers*.
Atwood, Margaret. "Face to Face." *Maclean's* May 1974: 38+. Rpt. in New
33–40.
Combines Atwood's personal response to Laurence with an interview.
_____ . Afterword. *A Jest of God*. By Margaret Laurence. New Canadian
Library. Toronto: McClelland 1988. 211–15.
Contemporary feminist perspective on the novel; a personal response.
Bevan, Allan. Introduction. *The Fire-Dwellers*. By Margaret Laurence. New
Canadian Library. Toronto: McClelland, 1973. viii–xiv. Rpt. in New 205–11.
Succinct and useful introduction to the novel.
Cameron, Donald. "Margaret Laurence: The Black Celt Speaks of Freedom."
Conversations with Canadian Novelists — I. Toronto: Macmillan, 1973.
96–115.
An important interview which includes discussion of Laurence's prairie
childhood, the autobiographical aspect of her fiction, her sense of history and
religion, the themes of freedom and isolation in her work.
Coger, Greta, ed. *Margaret Laurence: Fiction and Fact*. Westport: Greenwood,
forthcoming.
A varied and interesting collection of essays on Laurence's fiction.
Coldwell, Joan. "Laurence, Margaret." *The Oxford Companion to Canadian
Literature*. Ed. William Toye. Toronto: Oxford UP, 1983, 434–36.
Fraser, Sylvia. Afterword. *The Fire-Dwellers*. By Margaret Laurence. New
Canadian Library. Toronto: McClelland, 1988. 283–86.
A contemporary feminist perspective on the novel.
Gibson, Graeme. "Margaret Laurence." *Eleven Canadian Novelists*. Toronto:
Anansi, 1973. 181–208.
Includes Laurence's views on the form of the novel, the effect of film on
writers, the role of the writer in society, and the role of the woman writer.

Grosskurth, Phyllis. "Wise and Gentle." *Canadian Literature* 43 (1970): 91–92. Rpt. in New 194–96.

A review demonstrating sympathy with Stacey's plight.

Gunnars, Kristjana, ed. *Crossing the River: Essays in Honour of Margaret Laurence*. Winnipeg: Turnstone, 1988.

An interesting collection of articles on Laurence.

Hind-Smith, Joan. *Three Voices: The Lives of Margaret Laurence, Gabrielle Roy, Frederick Philip Grove*. Toronto: Clarke, 1975 1–60.

A useful review of Laurence's life until the mid-seventies.

Journal of Canadian Fiction 27 (1980).

Special issue on "The Work of Margaret Laurence."

Journal of Canadian Studies 13.3 (1978).

Special issue on Margaret Laurence.

Kattan, Naim. "Une Femme de Quarante Ans." *Le Devoir* 13 Sept. 1969. Rpt. in New 200–202.

An appreciative review of *The Fire-Dwellers* in French.

Kertzer, Jon. *Margaret Laurence and Her Works*. Toronto: ECW. n.d.

A perceptive and articulate, if brief, discussion of Laurence's fiction.

_____ . *Introducing Margaret Laurence's A Bird in the House*. Canadian Fiction Studies. Toronto: ECW, 1991.

Reader's guide to the novel.

Killam, G.D. Introduction. *A Jest of God*. By Margaret Laurence. New Canadian Library III. Toronto: McClelland, 1974. N. pag.

Discusses communication as Laurence's central theme.

Kroetsch, Robert. "A Conversation with Margaret Laurence." *Creation*. Ed. Robert Kroetsch. Toronto: New, 1970. 53–63. Rpt. in Woodcock 46–55.

Interview includes Kroetsch's and Laurence's views on writing, character, symbol, and their sense of the West.

Laurence, Margaret, ed. and trans. *A Bird in the House*. Toronto: McClelland, 1970. Stories.

_____ . *The Christmas Birthday Story*. Toronto: McClelland, 1980. Children's fiction.

_____ . *Dance on the Earth: A Memoir*. Toronto: McClelland, 1989.

_____ . *The Diviners*. Toronto: McClelland, 1974. Novel.

_____ . *The Fire-Dwellers*. Toronto: McClelland, 1969. Novel.

_____ . "Gadgetry or Growing: Form and Voice in the Novel." *Journal of Canadian Fiction* 27 (1980): 54–62. Rpt. in Woodcock 80–89. Essay.

_____ . *Heart of a Stranger*. Toronto: McClelland, 1976. Essays.

_____ . *Jason's Quest*. Toronto: McClelland, 1970. Children's fiction.

_____ . *A Jest of God*. Toronto: McClelland, 1966. Novel.

_____ . *Long Drums and Cannons: Nigerian Dramatists and Novelists 1952–1966*. London: Macmillan, 1968. Criticism.

———. *The Olden Days Coat*. Toronto: McClelland, 1979. Children's fiction.

———. *The Prophet's Camel Bell*. Toronto: McClelland, 1963. Journal.

———. *Six Darn Cows*. Toronto: Lorimer, 1979. Children's fiction.

———. *The Stone Angel*. Toronto: McClelland, 1964. Novel.

———. "Ten Years' Sentences." *Canadian Literature* 41 (1969): 10–16. Rpt. in New 17–23. Essay.

———. *This Side Jordan*. Toronto: McClelland, 1960. Novel.

———. "Time and the Narrative Voice." *The Narrative Voice*. Ed. John Metcalf. Toronto: McGraw-Hill, 1972. 126–30. Rpt. in New 156–60. Essay.

———. *The Tomorrow-Tamer*. Toronto: McClelland, 1963. Stories.

———, ed. and trans. *A Tree for Poverty: Somali Poetry and Prose*. Nairobi: Eagle, 1954. Translation.

Loercher, Diana. "Her Price for Coping." *The Christian Science Monitor*, 1969. Rpt. in New 203–04.
    Positive review.

Morley, Patricia. *Margaret Laurence*. Twayne's World Authors Ser. 591 Ed. Robert Lecker. Boston: G. K. Hall, 1981.
    A useful overview of Laurence's life and works. (rev. 1991)

Nancekevill, Sharon. "*The Fire-Dwellers*: Circles of Fire." *The Literary Criterion* 19 (1984): 158–72.
    Argues that the novel follows the heroic quest pattern demonstrated by Joseph Campbell in *The Hero with a Thousand Faces*.

New, William H., ed. *Margaret Laurence*. Critical Views on Canadian Writers Ser. Introduction by William New. Toronto: McGraw-Hill, 1977.
    Valuable collection of reviews, critical articles, and essays by Laurence.

Packer, Miriam. "The Dance of Life: *The Fire-Dwellers*." *Journal of Canadian Fiction* 27 (1980): 124–31.
    Enthusiastic discussion of Stacey's ultimate affirmation of life.

Spettigue, D. O. "Canadian Fiction." *Queen's Quarterly* 76 (1969): 722–24.
    Thoughtful review.

Stovel, Nora Foster. *Rachel's Children: Margaret Laurence's A Jest of God*. Canadian Fiction Studies. Toronto: ECW, 1991.
    Reader's guide to the novel.

———. "Sisters, Structures, and Symbols: *A Jest of God* and *The Fire-Dwellers*." *Margaret Laurence: Fiction and Fact*. Ed. Greta Coger. Westport: Greenwood's, forthcoming.
    Compares the two works in terms of character, theme, narrative structure and symbolism, demonstrating parallels between the sister novels.

———. *Wise Heart: A Biography of Margaret Laurence*. Canadian Biography Ser. ed. Robert Lecker. Toronto: ECW, forthcoming.

Thomas, Clara. *Margaret Laurence*. Canadian Writers Ser. 3. Toronto: McClelland, 1969.

General introduction which includes a chapter on *The Fire-Dwellers*.

_____ . *The Manawaka World of Margaret Laurence*. New Canadian Library 131. Toronto: McClelland, 1976.

Includes biographical information, analyses of the works, and discussions of Laurence's concern with the past, individual and cultural, and with place.

_____ . "The Novels of Margaret Laurence." *Studies in the Novel* 4.2 (1972): 154–64. Rpt. in New 55–65.

Discussion of Laurence's treatment of voice, time, and the journey motif.

Thompson, Kent. "Margaret Laurence: The Fire-Dwellers." *Fiddlehead* 82 (1969): 72–73.

Brief, thoughtful review.

Verduyn, Christl, ed. *Margaret Laurence: An Appreciation*. Peterborough: *Journal of Canadian Studies* and Broadview, 1988.

Interesting collection of articles on Laurence.

_____ . "Language, Body and Identity in Margaret Laurence's *The Fire-Dwellers*." *Margaret Laurence: An Appreciation. Journal of Canadian Studies*. Peterborough: Broadview, 1988: 128–40.

Contemporary feminist reading, linking language, body and identity.

Watt, Frank. "Review of *The Fire-Dwellers*." *Canadian Forum* July, 1969: 87. Rpt. in New 198–99.

Mixed review.

Warwick, Susan J. "A Laurence Log." *Journal of Canadian Studies* 13.3 (1978): 75–83.

Includes a chronology of Laurence's life to 1978 and a bibliography of books, articles, and theses on Laurence's work.

_____ . "Margaret Laurence: An Annotated Bibliography." *The Annotated Bibliography of Canada's Major Authors*. Ed. Robert Lecker and Jack David. Vol. 1. Downsview, Ont: ECW, 1979. 47–101.

_____ . *River of Now and Then: Margaret Laurence's The Diviners*. Canadian Fiction Studies. Toronto: ECW, 1991.

Reader's guide to the novel.

Woodcock, George, ed. *A Place to Stand On: Essays by and about Margaret Laurence*. Western Canadian Literary Documents Ser. 4. Edmonton: NeWest, 1983.

Valuable collection of articles by and about Margaret Laurence.

_____ . "The Human Elements: Margaret Laurence's Fiction." *The World of Canadian Writing*. Vancouver: Douglas, 49–62 (1980).

Argues that Laurence's Manawaka novels are each structured around one of the four elements.

_____ . *Introducing Margaret Laurence's The Stone Angel*. Canadian Fiction Studies. Toronto: ECW, 1989.

Useful reader's guide to the novel.

Index